Success, Motivation, and the Scriptures

Success, Motivation, and the Scriptures

William H. Cook

Broadman Press/Nashville, Tennessee

4252-26
ISBN: 0-8054-5226-5

Dewey Decimal Classification: 284.4
Library of Congress Catalog Card number: 74-82582
Printed in the United States of America

Foreword

For many years I have believed and have taught that Christians should be the most positive, the most attractive, and the most successful people in the world! Yet, many Christians are content to live humdrum, mediocre lives—content with the status quo when they could and should be turning the world "right-side up."

Many books have been written in recent years concerning how to be "successful." Too many of these, however, have been written from a humanistic point of view, leaving out the power of God and the spiritual dimension of life. Although many of the ideas presented have ultimately been derived from Christianity and the Bible, some of them are often contrary to the emphasis of the Bible. They are primarily influenced by the materialism of the society in which we live.

Christians find it difficult to evaluate such books. They have often either disregarded them as totally contrary to Scripture, and thus irrelevant; or they have adopted all of the principles, to the compromise of their faith.

The Christian alone possesses the enabling power of the Holy Spirit to live life to the fullest, as God designed it to be lived. This book does an excellent job of relating the ideas of success and positive motivation to the power of God and the work of the Holy Spirit.

Christians will find *Success, Motivation, and the Scriptures* helpful in evaluating other books written on success, and they will also find in it many practical benefits in areas such as: self-image, vision, faith, and goal-setting. The reader who applies the suggestions offered in this book, must get ready for an exciting adventure in Christian living.

BILL BRIGHT

Introduction

A work of this kind has been needed for a long time, but at no time has it been needed more than now!

The word that keeps pervading through my mind as I have read this volume is "balance."

Our adversary would divide us by leading us to suppose that aspirations to succeed and humility were enemies; that the Holy Spirit deplores personal motivation; and that positive thinking is an enemy of total commitment.

Bill Cook, in this superbly written work, not only refutes this and exposes it as falsehood, but shows in an exciting fashion how God fits seeming opposites together for his glory.

"Exciting" is the word which describes the manner in which the book is written.

"Exciting" is the word which describes the experience of the reader as he moves through these pages.

And even more exciting will be the future of anyone who applies the concepts revealed here.

Here is a fresh look at an old problem and a Spirit-anointed approach to its solution.

Aside from its thrilling thrust, there are enough pertinent illustrations to make the book more than worthwhile to anyone.

In a decade of walking in the realm of the Spirit-controlled life, I have not read a volume which has excited me more. It is a help to me. I commend it to you.

Jack R. Taylor

Author's Introduction

Yes, sir, God wants exciting success achieved through your life!

Provided, of course, your definition is correct. Like so many others, you may not have arrived. This book is designed to help you get there.

One of the big problems is that the very man who most desires to be successful has real trouble getting God on his side. Not that he should have trouble in this area, but he just hasn't figured out how to get the power of God going in his behalf. And to date, success books have not offered any solution to the problem. In fact, the author of one of the best known books has suggested there is a real difficulty not yet solved.

Dr. Maxwell Maltz, author of *Psycho-Cybernetics*, spelled out the dilemma a few years back. In 1969, at a time when his book on success had already sold 5 million copies, Dr. Maltz was speaking to a group in Dallas. Following the speech, he fielded questions from the audience. The question came, "Are spiritual-cybernetics the same as psycho-cybernetics?"

"Certainly not," Dr. Maltz replied. "The churches certainly seem to like my book. It teaches a great many things they teach—but mine is practical, everyday living which does not, incidentally, fit perfectly with religious concepts" (Dallas *Times-Herald*, Oct. 2, 1969).

No wonder so many are frustrated. As long as man cannot make practical success ideas blend perfectly with his spiritual side, he is in trouble.

Man swims in a sea where the accent is heavy, both on success and spirituality. Part of the time he enjoys his swim. But when both of the seemingly opposing sides pull on him at the same time, he wants to make like a tadpole, sprout his legs, and jump! Anything to get out of there for awhile.

Most of our wrestling matches come in three areas: (1) the success area; (2) the motivation area, and (3) the spiritual area. If it were possible to master these three fields, we would enjoy life to the fullest. Where these ideas cannot be correctly assimilated into a successful life of thrilling achievement, problems pyramid.

In our current situation, proponents of success and proponents of the spiritual life have fought to a standoff. On the one hand, there is the success-bug who has never figured out how to maintain his success-image and still be spiritual. So he concludes, wrongfully, that his is the only team really in the ball game. On the other end of the field is the individual who views his relationship with God as being of prime importance. He is suspicious of accepting new ideas about success and motivation until he is sure they do not rob him of what he already has. So the life of maximum achievement God intended never seems to bounce in his direction.

As in any standoff, both sides lose. This book is dedicated to the idea that it need not be that way—that the individual who correctly assimilates success, motivation, and the truths of Scripture is in for fantastic excitement and achievement.

Contents

PART ONE:
PROBLEMS WITH SUCCESS AND ACHIEVEMENT

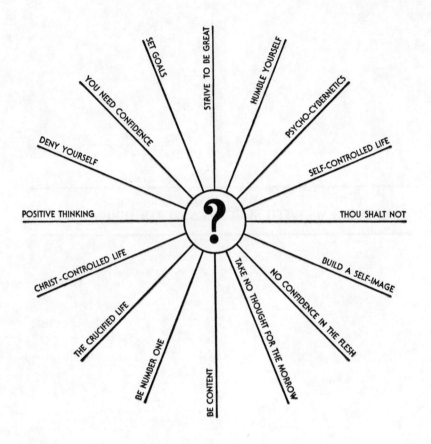

1
WRESTLING WITH THE SUCCESS QUESTION

Someone better tie success and the spiritual together.

Success salesmen aren't carrying the day. They are well aware they reach only a small percentage of the market. And of that percentage, only a few really succeed.

Christians aren't carrying the day either. The percentage of the world population considered thrilling, well-adjusted, achieving Christians is not very large at all.

The rest of the world sits off skeptically observing. That percentage (probably more than half of the people) won't buy success principles which fail to relate to the spiritual side of life, and they want nothing to do with a Christianity that can't tell them how to be successful.

God, are you interested or not interested in my being successful? Voices are coming at me from every side. I'm coming apart at the seams. I've got to know!

The problem is that everybody seems to tell us something different. That makes frustration really grow. For instance, should I

Set goals

or do I decide to

Take no thought for the morrow?

One voice tells me I need a

Self-controlled life

and another says I need a

Christ-controlled life.

I picked up a good book that described me perfectly when it said

You need confidence

but doesn't the Bible say

Have no confidence in the flesh?

My friend encouraged me to
  Build a self-image
      yet Jesus taught that a man should
          Deny himself.
Just as I was about to master
  Positive thinking
          my mind remembered negative commandments
          saying
              Thou shalt not.
Then I heard an outstanding lecturer say I should
  Strive to be great
          yet Dad always quoted a Bible verse
              Be content with such things as ye have.
How can I
  Be Number One
      and at the same time
          Humble myself in the sight of God.
Frankly, I just love
  Psycho-Cybernetics
      but how would it relate to
          The crucified life?
Frustrating, isn't it? Just about the time the brain gets loaded
with exciting ideas, we become aware of a conflict. These
concepts may seem exciting, but they just don't seem to go
together.

One Problem or Many?

Before an attempt can be made at reconciling the different
ideas, one needs to decide whether he is wrestling with eight
problems or one. Study the diagram on page 4 again. Is it
not possible that these are but eight facets of the same problem? For, in reality, eight ideas of the Scripture are presented
in the diagram, contrasting with eight ideas generally considered to bring success and produce motivation.

One who views the diagram might readily conclude that
the Bible places "thumbs down on success." Another could

assume that success books totally repudiate the Bible. Neither assumption is correct. In fact, the Bible is remarkably full of "success ideas." And instead of the biblical ideas degrading the eight success thoughts of the diagram, there may be some remarkable proximity.

The problem is that man has never learned to reconcile success and the spiritual. There have been thousands of books dealing with the spiritual, and a great number dealing with success, but apparently no one has sensed the need for tying the two together. No one except frustrated man.

The Difficulty Observed

The human brain is somewhat like a giant smelter. Contrasting ideas can be thrown in, and some type of finished product will surely emerge. But the finished product emerging from the success-spiritual hopper is not always pleasant to behold. Lives have been torn apart simply due to a weakness in reconciliation.

For instance, one man repudiates success. Being a Bible believer, his subconscious goes through the daily ritual of "What I can't find in the Bible, I omit." The danger comes at the point where the Bible is brimful of a particular subject and he simply has not discovered it. It is a false assumption for him to conclude, "If I'm spiritual, then I'm not supposed to be successful."

The next man may repudiate the Bible. He lives and works in a world so success-oriented that he considers he has no choice. Certainly he cannot drop the success ideas pounded into his brain at the office. To repudiate the ideas would be to lose his livelihood, and since the Bible doesn't directly contribute to his "making a living," it is far easier to negate the Bible. Not that he has studied the Bible with relation to success, because he hasn't. But not having heard a sermon on it yet, he assumes it's just not in there. So Mr. Businessman chalks off the Bible as relatively unimportant, thinking to himself, "If I really want to be a success, I must avoid trends toward spirituality."

A third man may be in the saddest predicament of all. He has assumed, "God is not interested in me, particularly my success." This man has a warped idea of God; God is a God who deprives of pleasure, rather than giving it, takes away joy instead of being the cause of it. So he struggles along in his own power, most of the time defeated, with his head pointed down in dejection. "I don't expect God to get interested in doing anything for me; he just tells me what *not* to do," the reasoning goes.

Results of the Failure to Reconcile

If one cannot correctly reconcile his concepts of success and the spiritual, he faces immediate frustration. Frequently the frustration comes about four weeks after reading his first success book. The thought finally dawns, "Wait a minute, I'm not sure I understand how all that fits in with the Bible." Result—well, just like the centipede!

> The centipede was quite happy
> Until a frog in fun
> Said, "Pray, which leg goes after which?"
> That worked her mind to such a pitch
> She lay distracted in a ditch
> Considering how to run.

The other result is schizophrenia. The best illustration may be the story of the farmer who had been taken by the car salesman so many times that he was geared and ready when the salesman wanted to buy a cow. The farmer priced it, "basic cow, $200; two-tone extra, $45; extra stomach, $75; produce storage compartment, $60; dispensing device, four spigots at $10 each, $40; genuine cowhide upholstery, $125; dual horns, $15; automatic fly swatter, $35; total—$595."

Failure to correctly reconcile ideas of success with ideas of the spiritual life will give man a centipede complex or make him feel like a segmented cow! And no wonder! One man "escapes" by subdividing himself into a Sunday morning personality versus a rest-of-the-week personality. Without knowing why, another will develop a business personality (where he pretends to be the picture of success) and a home personality (where he's a real bear!). Another becomes so schizophrenic as to have six or seven personalities he turns on—depending on where he is and who he is with.

Needless to say, when man cannot assimilate and be the one total successful and spiritual personality God intended, he is in trouble. But if he ever turns the key—if correct concepts of success, motivation, and the Scriptures are assimilated into an individual's life, there will emerge a life filled with enthusiasm and excitement.

Concepts for Excitement

With strong conviction that God has something better for us than the centipede complex, I offer what I choose to call, six concepts for excitement.

1. God is interested in your being successful, provided your definition of success is right.
2. God should know more about success than anyone who has ever written on the subject.
3. God put man into the world to succeed, not fail.
4. God is interested in goals—interested in helping you formulate some that would benefit you tremendously.
5. God has written a book and shared within its pages some excellent principles of success.
6. God knows more about how to motivate man than any other authority in the field. Once he helps in the formulation of our goals, he then provides inner motivation for maximum achievement.

2
THE CRAVING FOR SUCCESS—
AND THE OBSTACLES

> Honey, God don't sponsor no flops.
> —Ethel Waters

> For then thou shalt make thy way prosperous, and
> then thou shalt have good success.
> —God to Joshua
> Joshua 1:8

How's your success craving? It is probably safe to say that most everyone possesses an inner craving for success. Most of us accept it without a second thought, although an occasional few might consider such a craving sinful. The question is, "Is it right to want to be successful?"

Before answering that one, let's consider a definition of success. One dictionary calls it "the satisfactory accomplishment of a goal sought for." Later we shall seek to establish a definition perhaps even more satisfactory, but for now, let's stick to that one. And let's analyze our craving.

Psychology Speaks on Success

Most of us just know we would like to be successful. We are not sure why. We just know we want to be. Psychology (the study of human behavior and animal behavior) goes farther than that. Psychology says you don't just want to be, you have to be. Your system demands it.

Writing as far back as 1929, Dr. William Burnham, in a chapter entitled "Success As a Stimulus," suggests:

The need of success as a wholesome stimulus is universal. Children have an enormous appetite for it. They need large doses. Adults become depressed without. It is vital for the normal. The diseased are often cured by it. The modern method in the best hospitals of giving the patient as far as possible interesting work, something worth while to do, has demonstrated its value for health. It is the gravest error for physicians, social workers, and teachers not to employ this stimulus.[1]

Achievement and accomplishment are inbred desires. There is definitely a dream of success in the human brain. Man can be analyzed, or admonished and nothing happens. He may even be approved, appreciated, and acclaimed, and the personality remains stifled. But if man can honestly feel deep within that he has achieved, his personality comes alive.

Study the small child from the time he begins to play in the crib. He is interested in one thing—satisfactory accomplishment of a goal sought for. If he cannot accomplish his goals, however small they may be, he is miserable. He craves success, exactly as the dictionary defines it. Surely that's no sin, but simply the following of an inbred God-given desire.

Analyzing the Obstacles

Because man has an inbred desire for success from the time he is born, then it should be easy to attain—right?

Wrong.

The reason success is never easy to obtain is because there are several obstacles in the way. Too, each obstacle has to do with an attitude, and attitudes are never easy to change. However, changes come easier after honest confrontation.

The "I may not succeed, but it's because I live in the toughest times ever" attitude.—It is probably safe to say that some have used that as their argument for do-nothingness in every generation since the days of Jesus.

Honesty would reveal that in some ways, the times we live in are the greatest ever. Other generations did not possess half the opportunities we have. There is a vast difference between great times and easy times, and while our times are not easy, they are definitely great. The days reek with outstanding accomplishment. Some have estimated that 90 percent of all the world's knowledge since the days of Adam and

Eve has been gained in our day. Whatever the statistic, the increase in knowledge while we have been alive has been astounding.

To view our times in another light, nine out of every ten scientists who have ever lived are alive right now. No, honesty forces us to admit that we are not living in the toughest times ever, but the best times ever. These are times of challenge, yes, but also the greatest times of all history.

This makes it a good time to consider, "What am I doing here? Why is it that I'm alive now, instead of having lived centuries ago?"

The alternatives are only two. Either God blundered or he knew exactly what he was doing in allowing us to live in the twentieth century. If he did not blunder, then God has matched us with this generation. He must have thought there was the potential of accomplishing exactly what needed to be accomplished in the twentieth-century world through us, or he made a mistake in not preserving some of the giants of the past for this day. Knowing God makes no mistakes, our lives should be wonderfully alive with excitement.

The "But I don't have any motivation" attitude.—Goal-striving man has a real problem at this point, mainly because he usually seeks motivation in the wrong place. The individual who must always be motivated from without is in trouble. When the boss is around to push him hard, he becomes an achiever. But when the boss is not around. . . .

When the raise is considered "big enough" or the order is given "loud enough," he moves. In some cases, action comes only when he is assaulted by fear.

Of course, the best motivation is motivation from within. And who, do you suppose, knows the most about that?

The "Okay, I need it, but does God want me to have it?" *attitude.*—This last-mentioned attitude may be the biggest hangup yet. After all, who needs to accomplish anything as long as he can blame God for his nonaccomplishment? The person who decides he is "just like God made him" has, he thinks, an excellent excuse for his laziness. It has never dawned on him that Jesus (in the parable of the talents) emphasized the necessity of the individual producing increase.

I may say to myself, "There are many things more important than success" or "I haven't achieved much, but I have a great family!" Another excuse I could use is "I just consider it more important to be something than to have something."

Isn't it tragic, though, when I pull a true statement out of my hat and use it to excuse myself for being less than what God intended me to be!

God simply did not create man to come in second place.

God Has More

During my first year of college, browsing through the library one day, I chanced upon an old book entitled *Service*. One illustration from the book has stuck in my memory to this day. Inflation has long since ruined the price factor, but not the message of the story.

If you were to see a piece of iron in a junkyard, that iron would be worth about $1\frac{1}{2}$ cent per pound. The same iron, however, could be heated and made into other objects much more valuable. If the iron was fashioned and

made into a steam engine, its value would be 7 cents per pound.

made into a mould-board for a plow, 15 cents per pound.

made into scissors or razors, 25 cents per pound.

made into needles, $25 per pound.

made into medical instruments, $100 per pound.

made into a tiny watch-part, $500 per pound.

I find it incredible for some to think that God would want them lying in the junkyard with everything else that's mediocre. We desperately need new vision to see how much more valuable our lives can become.

------

[1] Reprinted by permission of Hawthorn Books, Inc., from *The Normal Mind* by William H. Burnham. Copyright © 1929 by D. Appelton & Co. All rights reserved.

3
SUCCESS IMAGE; FAILURE IMAGE?

Someone asked George Beverly Shea how much
he knew about God. He said, "Not much, but what
I do know has changed my life."
—Billy Graham

Are we to believe that the same God who en-
gineered a successful creation, gave man a successful human body, assigned man tasks which
demanded success, stamped man's brain with a
failure image?

Nineteen hundred and sixty-six was the year of the atten-
tion-getting best seller, *Psycho-Cybernetics*. Dr. Maxwell
Maltz, brilliant plastic surgeon, became an author because
he could not escape sharing some observations he made after
he removed scars from his patients.

His description? "Some patients show no change in personality after surgery. In most cases a person who had a conspic-
uously ugly face, or some 'freakish' feature corrected by surgery, experiences an almost immediate (usually within 21 days)
rise in self-esteem, self-confidence. But in some cases, the
patient continued to feel inadequate and experienced feelings
of inferiority. In short, these 'failures' continued to feel, act
and behave just as if they still have an ugly face." [1]

After studying patients over a period of time, Dr. Matlz
concluded that some have success "instincts." Others feel
doomed to failure—possess failure instincts—and consequently, these invariably fail.

Nobody really wants to admit to possessing a failure instinct.
However, most would admit having a mediocrity image. In
reality, a mediocrity image is nothing more than a masked
failure image. If Maltz is right in his conclusion at this point
(we shall analyze other concepts of his later), you either have

a success image or a failure image. You are definitely not a Mr. In-Between.

Let's tell it like it is. If you stare into the mirror each morning, having no meaningful goals for the day, not even expecting to accomplish anything except routine things, you have a failure image! You may rise in indignation to protest that you are a Bible-believing Christian, but the truth still stands—you have a failure image. You are expecting nothing meaningful from the day, envisioning no great accomplishments, and you will get exactly what you expect.

Success and Creation

It might help at the outset to just admit that you did not get your failure image (or mediocrity image, if that term makes you feel better) from God. What God does is never mediocre—but wonderfully successful!

There is a wonderful excitement even in the oft-heard story of creation. The first chapter of Genesis exclaims: "And God saw the light, that it was good" (1:4). "And God called the dry land Earth; and the gathering together of the waters called he Seas; and God saw that it was good" (v. 10).

Later God commanded the grass to grow and the trees to yield fruit, and it was good (v. 12). When the sun and moon appeared in the sky, thrust there by the Almighty himself, God saw that it was good (v. 18). Creative activity continued with the cattle of the field and the beasts of the earth and again God saw that it was good (1:25).

God's success ability is further explained by Dr. Walter Wilson. He does an excellent job of describing the greatness of creation in his little tract "Wonders of Nature."

An unbeliever once said, "I will believe only what I can understand; none of that mystery stuff for me."

He was asked to explain this problem: How is it possible for a black cow to eat green grass which makes white milk and churns yellow butter?

Can you explain this mystery of God? Note some other mysteries of His creation.

Consider the remarkable transformation that takes place when a caterpillar (an upholstered worm) encases itself in its homemade casket and is changed into a beautiful butterfly. Its hair is changed to scales—a million to the square inch; the many legs of the caterpillar become the six legs of the butterfly; the yellow becomes a beautiful red; the crawling instinct becomes a flying instinct.

Thus will God take the life of a sinner and transform it until it glows with the beauty of the Lord and is fragrant with the graces of Heaven.

A handful of sand is deposited by the Lord in the heart of the earth. Great heat is applied from beneath and ponderous weight from above until, when it is found by man, it has been miraculously changed into a beautiful, fiery opal.

God takes a handful of black carbon, plants it deep in the bowels of the earth, treats it with heat below, presses it with rocks of the mountains above, and transforms it into a glorious diamond fit for a king's crown.

As God performs these wonderful miracles in nature, He also can transform the souls of men and renew their hearts if they only trust fully in Christ Jesus, the Lord of life.

God knows how to regulate nature. Only the One who made you can successfully direct you. Only the One who made your brain and your heart can successfully guide them to a profitable end.

God's wisdom is seen in the structure of the elephant. The four legs of this great beast bend forward in the same direction. No other quadruped is so made. God planned that this animal should have a huge body, too large to live on two legs. For this reason He gave it four fulcrums so that it could rise from the ground easily.

God's wisdom is revealed in His arrangements of sections and segments as well as in the number of grains.

Each watermelon has an even number of stripes on the rind.

Each orange has an even number of segments.

Each stalk of wheat has an even number of grains.

Another mystery as yet unsolved by man is this: God causes the trunk of a tree to grow straight out from the trunk for a distance of forty, fifty, or sixty feet, with no other anchorage than fifteen or eighteen inches of fibers which lose themselves in the trunk of the tree. No human being has discovered how to apply this principle in the construction of buildings or bridges.

God takes oxygen and hydrogen, both of them odorless, tasteless, and colorless, and combines them with carbon which is insoluble, black and tasteless. The result of this combination is beautiful, white, sweet sugar. How does God do it? I do not understand.

I know only that God can take your life—drab, useless and fruitless—and transform it into a beautiful garden of the sweetest graces for His glory. He will do this for you, if you will trust your life to Him! [2]

Success and the First Man

The same God who pioneered success with the first five days of created activity personalized success on the sixth day.

He thrust into a shell of skin some 263 bones, and wrapped them in 500 muscles. He perfected a little heart six inches in length, and only four inches in diameter that would beat

>70 times a minute
>>4,200 times an hour
>>>100,800 times a day
>>>>36,792,000 times a year
>>>>>and 2,575,440,000 times in 70 years.

So successful was the little heart that everytime it would beat it would pump blood at the rate of

>2½ ounces per beat
>>175 ounces per minute
>>>656 pounds an hour
>>>>and 7 and ¾ tons in one day.

Small wonder that the psalmist would rejoice and say, "I will praise thee, for I am fearfully and wonderfully made."

Success and "God's Image"

For man to be content to be mediocre is not pleasing to God. Though the end result of achievement is different with different individuals, no man must be content to be less than God's best. Success is not measured by what we are. It is measured by what we are compared to what we could be.

At the outset, the first man Adam was all he could be. Before sin entered, he was totally in the image of God.

What does that mean? Dr. Walter Thomas Conner is enlightening at this point.

"We are told in Genesis 1:26, 27 that God made man in his own image and likeness. What does this expression mean? . . . in what respects is man like God? . . . what are some of the essential functions or powers that belong to man as a spiritual personality?" [3]

Then Dr. Conner answers his own question:

(1) The first that should be mentioned is intelligence or the power to think—The lower animals possess this power in a very crude and elementary sense. Man has the power to know. . . .

(2) The second thing is the power of rational affection—The lower animals have sensibility and instinctive affection. But man rises above the lower animals as much in his life of sensibility and affection as he does in his thought life. Rational love is the highest moral quality in God and in man. . . .

(3) The third thing is free will—Man is a free being. He has the power of self-determination. He can be influenced but not forced. In this respect he is like God. God is the only perfectly free being in the universe. . . . Man's freedom is limited but real. He has the power to form ideals and then to direct his energies toward the attainment of those ideals. . . .

(4) Another respect in which man is like God is in the possession of the moral sense—In the general use of the term, that is what is meant by conscience. Man has the innate sense of right and wrong [4]

Note that every one of the four aspects of personality is a success necessity designed to point man in an upward direction.

But there is another side to the "Image of God." A. H. Strong suggests, "In what did the image of God consist? We reply that it consisted in (1) Natural likeness to God, or personality; (2) Moral likeness to God, or holiness." [5] Have you ever summarized the first man with the mathematical process of addition?

4 success necessities (listed above)
+ 1 moral likeness to God
SUCCESS

Man was so designed that the only way failure could gain entrance to his life was for him to consider some plan other than the plan of God and some other will other than the will of God.

God preceded man with success, challenged man by success, prepared man for success, and then presented man his own image. Success was not man's doing, but God's!

This might be an excellent place for a multiple choice test question. In your mind's eye, circle either the (a) or (b).

Question—God expected Adam to have
      (a) A success image?
      (b) A failure image?

---

[1] Maxwell Maltz, M.D., *Psycho-Cybernetics* (Englewood Cliffs, N.J.: Prentice Hall, Inc., 1960), p. vi. Used by permission.

[2] Reprinted by permission from a tract, Good news Publishers, Westchester, Illinois 60153.

[3] W. T. Conner, *Revelation and God: An Introduction to Christian Doctrine* (Nashville: Broadman Press, 1936, Renewal, 1964), p. 51. Used by permission.

[4] *Ibid.*, pp. 51-52.

[5] A. H. Strong, *Systematic Theology* (Philadelphia: Judson Press, 1907), p. 514.

4
THE BIBLICAL BEGINNING OF A FAILURE-IMAGE

U.S. Industry has a new generation of problem children—workers with the blue collar blues and the white collar blahs (*Newsweek*, March 26, 1973).

Of course God wants us to succeed in the task he has given us. He wants us to be mightily motivated, full of confidence, excited about life.

Now let's talk about defects. How about a moment of honest appraisal?

"On their honeymoon, the groom took his bride by the hand and said, 'Now that we're married, dear, I hope you won't mind if I mention a few little defects that I've noticed about you.'

'Not at all,' the bride replied with a deceptive sweetness. 'It was those little defects that kept me from getting a better husband.' "

Those little defects—those irritating little defects—are a very real part of each of us. We try to laugh it off by emphasizing our good aspects. For instance, if I'm certain God is interested in the total me (chap. 1), if I'm thoroughly convinced I could be more successful than I am (chap. 2), and if I have no problem believing God stamped the first man with a success-image (chap. 3), then it's easy to brag on myself, "I don't have any hangups at all!" Except maybe a few little defects.

On close examination it is evident that something has happened to the successful person God created. For instance, each of us could ask: "Where do I get my negative ideas about success? Why do I always have to be pushed? Sometimes it seems I have no motivation at all. How is it that I can feel so successful one day and so like a failure the next? Why is

24

it that so many things about my life are not pleasing to God?"

Tough question—real tough. And the questions are not made any easier by the discussion about man in the image of God. If I'm in God's image, shouldn't I be an outstanding success? Shouldn't I have a success image like the first man? Then why the blue-collar blues or the white-collar blahs?

Adam and Modern Man

Who said you were in God's image? That was Adam, remember?

The mistaken idea that each of us is automatically in God's image could have come from several sources. Perhaps when the minister's sermon mentioned God's image, the mind believed what it wanted to believe and an inner voice said, "That's me!" Or occasionally the idea has been advanced by a success author, usually the author who ignored God through the first two thirds of his book.

At any rate, the idea that modern secular man is in the image of God is only half right. In the last chapter we learned that the image of God consisted of both a natural likeness and a moral likeness.

Every man has a .500 batting average, because every man has a natural likeness to God (personality). He still has intelligence, or the power to think; power of rational affection; power to form ideals and direct energies toward attainment; innate sense of right and wrong.

Splendid! But only so far as it goes. Since man was created not only with that natural likeness but also a moral likeness to God, we suddenly discover the cause of our defects.

We can possess all aspects of the natural likeness but if there is no moral likeness we cannot truthfully say we are in God's image. And when we are honest, we admit that in the moral area (holiness), someone has been tampering with us. We have computer trouble. Consequently, it is not unusual for some of us to possess either an outright failure-image or a not-much-better mediocrity image.

How the Success Image Got Tarnished

According to the Bible, there are two supernatural powers, each thoroughly capable of brain programming.

Programmer A always thrusts in excitement and thrill and purpose. This is the one who challenged man by success, created man in success, appointed man over success and prepared man for success. Adam, after receiving that kind of input, thought, "Great!"

Not very far down the road of success Adam met Programmer B. Now remember that up to this point Adam was programmed right and motivated right. As long as he would stick with God he was bound for success. He would achieve everything God intended for him to achieve, meet every goal in God's plan for his life, and enjoy life to the hilt.

Programmer B suggested he had a better mousetrap! "I can give you new insights, new knowledge—just come my way," Satan suggested. So Adam received new knowledge (wrong kind), new insights (became sin-oriented) and to top it all lost the one thing which had made him supremely happy. His fellowship with God was suddenly nil. Programmer B (Satan) had filled the mind with wrong information and computer foul-up resulted.

From then until now, man has had difficulty in both success and motivation. While desiring to be continually motivated toward success, he knows there are weaknesses within.

Before God can move in and correct the weaknesses, it might be necessary for us to examine some of our basic concepts which influence our entire philosophy of success.

PART TWO:
A TIME FOR QUESTIONS

5
HOW MUCH MONEY SHOULD A CHRISTIAN MAKE?

> Make all you can,
>   save all you can
>   give all you can.
>
> —John Wesley

> Money has never made a man happy yet, nor will
> it. There is nothing in its nature to produce happi-
> ness. The more a man has, the more he wants.
> Instead of its filling a vacuum, it makes one. If
> it satisfies one want, it doubles and trebles that
> want another way. That was a true proverb of
> the wise man, rely upon it: "Better is little with
> the fear of the Lord, than great treasure, and
> trouble therewith."
>
> —Benjamin Franklin.

Jesus told a story about a rich man (Luke 12:13-21) and the man's main emphasis was on MY crops, MY barns, MY grain, and MY goods. God stepped in to assure him he had less than twenty-four hours to live, and commented, "Thou fool!"

The money question and the selfishness that generally goes with it has ruined many a person along the route to success. Other major questions are involved (questions about success books, proper success definitions, and the question of how to feel successful). But the question more people think about is the money question. How does money relate to success? Does it relate at all? Is money the root of all evil? Is it just a necessary evil? Is it evil at all? What should be the relation of a Christian to money-making?

A Christian Should Make Money

The Bible definitely teaches that money-making is to be

a part of the life of a follower of God.

Recently one of the nation's newsmagazines talked about a new fad among youth. The fad—to not believe in work.

That's not hard to figure. Some young people, noting how the older generation has worshiped money, have gone to the opposite extreme. But we must not ignore the Bible command, "Six days shalt thou labour" (Ex. 20:9).

There's nothing new under the sun! Ancient Thessalonica is an excellent example to prove our twentieth-century thinking is 19 centuries out of date.

Thessalonica had some Christians who believed that Jesus would come soon. They formed a "Let's-Just-Wait-for-the-Second Coming" group. And they would not work! They wanted to sit on the highest mountain and watch for the return of Christ. They wouldn't even earn enough money to feed themselves. The Thessalonica Welfare Department could take care of that!

Through Paul, God thundered his commandment. "Work with your own hands as we commanded; that ye may walk honestly toward them that are without, and that ye may have lack of nothing." *The Living Bible* reads, "Doing your own work, just as we told you before. As a result, people who are not Christians will trust and respect you, and you will not need to depend on others for enough money to pay your bills" (1 Thess. 4:11-12).[1]

Paul's letter fell on deaf ears to some in the church. So when Paul wrote a second letter to them, he made it even stronger. "For even when we were with you, this we commanded you, that if any would not work, neither should he eat. For we hear that there are some which walk among you disorderly, working not at all, but are busybodies. Now them that are such we command and exhort by our Lord Jesus Christ, that with quietness they work, and eat their own bread" (2 Thess. 3:10-12).

There is only one type of life for a Christian to live—and the making of money through honest work is a vital part of it.

But How Much?

A question most of us have thought about but few of us have dared to ask is, "How much money should a Christian make?" Can I expect God's favor if I make a lot of money?

Dr. B. H. Carroll, in *An Interpretation of the English Bible*, is stimulating at this point. He asks, " 'Just how rich does the New Testament allow a Christian to become?' Or, what is the New Testament's limit to the amount of wealth a Christian may lawfully acquire?" [2]

In my early pastorate at Waco I put this very question to my Sunday school, to be answered the following week. There chanced to be present a millionaire from Newark, New Jersey, who had made his money in Texas, Morgan L. Smith. He approached me when the school was dismissed saying that the question interested him personally, and he would leave before the following Sunday, would take it as a favor if I would give him the answer in advance.

I read to him this passage from 3 John: "Beloved, I pray that in all things thou mayest prosper and be in health, even as thy soul prospereth," which I thus interpreted: John would not pray for unlawful things. He did pray that Gaius might prosper financially just as far as was consistent with his prosperity of soul. Therefore, it was lawful to acquire a million, ten million, any number of millions, if the acquisition did no harm to the soul.

But in many cases wealth as gained or as used starved and sickened the soul. To them any amount was unlawful that worked such result. It was good for such men that God kept them poor; if he allowed to them an increase of wealth at the expense of the soul, it was in anger and as a judgment. Prosperity makes fools of many. The same law applied to health. Some could be well all the time and the soul the better for it. Others, like Jeshurun, kicked when they waxed fat. Many may echo the Bible statement, "Before I was afflicted I went astray." [3]

God is apparently not interested in helping anyone run off and leave his spirituality. If the financial goal-setter wants God on his side, let him be certain this facet of his life is under the complete control of Jesus Christ.

Ways Money Ruins

Our materialistic orientation has never wanted to let us consider the fact that money can ruin. And some of us have never considered it because we've never had enough to have to think about it! There are at least five ways, however, in which money can ruin.

1. *Too much money can ruin one's goals.*—Worthy goals become lost. Goals of service and goals of sacrifice fall by the wayside. The one consuming passion—"I must figure ways to make more money."

2. *Too much money can ruin one's family.*—In this case, the individual can stand it, but his kids cannot. Either in teenage years, or at twenty-one, the money Dad provided ruins them.

3. *Climbing the money ladder can destroy character and morals.*—The man who is a "climber" may be so anxious to climb and "have it made" that the people he used and manipulated in his climb can't stand to be around him now. With another man, character may succumb to outright evil. Morality disappears due to the influence of the money he has. Man will always seek to rename his sin under the guise of a "new morality" (exactly identical to the old immorality in God's sight) but the result is the same. Character is destroyed.

4. *Too much money may thwart God's purpose for the life.*—Ever dream of building a big house on a high hill? Who hasn't! What's the motive? Escape? Get away from people? Hide from human need? "Woe unto him that coveteth an evil covetousness to his house, that he may set his nest on high, that he may be delivered from the power of evil! Thou hast consulted shame to thy house by cutting off many people, and has sinned against thy soul" (Hab. 2:9-10). Seclusion, whether in a monastery or a "home of my dreams"—that which gets you farther and farther from the people who need you— just doesn't seem to be God's perfect will.

5. *Too much money may result in ego-inflation.*—"Look

what *I* did. Let me tell you how *I* made it!" Reread the opening paragraph of this chapter. See any similarities?

God Knows Best

One day it dawned on me that God knew better than I just exactly how much money it would take to ruin me. It was incredible that I (or any Christian) would set a monetary goal and not bathe it in prayer. Believing that God is wonderfully interested in me, and my success for his glory, why should I worry about what I don't have? I ought to thank God daily that he has never been interested in helping me attain so much that my life would be ruined by what I had attained. The one who is yielded and usable can always thank God regardless of the amount of money he has. He can set his goals and strive for them, once he is convinced they are God's goals for his life. Regardless of the amount he possesses, let him trust God's judgment.

Maybe God needs you where you are! God needs highly successful people in each income bracket of society.

For example, take the lower income bracket. Don't you suppose God needs successful people in that bracket to show others without much income how they should live? Wouldn't the same be true of the lower-middle income bracket? The middle bracket? The upper-middle? And isn't it reasonable to believe God wants some Christian millionaries who are highly successful in life as well as money? A millionaire commented to me, "The most depraved men I know are millionaires."

If God put all successful people in the upper income bracket, and if God reserved success only for these, then the other 98 percent of the world's population would never know what it meant to be successful.

The Danger of Greed

"Charge them that are rich in this world that they be not highminded, nor trust in uncertain riches, but in the living

God, who giveth us richly all things to enjoy; that they do good, that they be rich in good works, ready to distribute, willing to communicate; laying up in store for themselves a good foundation against the time to come, that they may lay hold an eternal life" (1 Tim. 6:17-19).

Money is not the root of all evil. Of itself, money is neutral. But the Bible says that the love of money (human greed) is the root of all evil (v. 10). It is impossible to warn too much against the dangers of that.

Tolstoi has a powerful story of a young Russian who fell heir to his father's small farm. He was no sooner in possession of this land than he began to dream eagerly, of how he could add to it. One morning a stranger, evidently a person of great power and authority, came to him and told him, as they were standing near the old homestead, that he could have, for nothing, all the land he could walk over in one day—but at sundown he must be back at the very place from which he started. Pointing to the grave of this young man's father, the stranger said, "This is the point to which you must return."

The youth looked eagerly over the rich fields in the distance and throwing off his coat and without waiting to say a word to his wife and children, started off across the fields. His first plan was to cover the tract of ground 6 miles square; but when he had walked the six he decided to make it 9, then 12, then 15—which would give him 60 miles before sundown!

By noon he had covered 2 sides of this square of 30 miles. But eager to get on and compass the whole distance, he did not stop for food. An hour later he saw an old man drinking at a spring, but in his hunger for land he brushed aside the cup which the old man offered and rushed on in his eager quest for possession of land. When he was a few miles from the goal he was worn down with fatigue.

A few hundred yards from the line he saw the sun approaching the horizon and knew that he had but a few minutes left. Hurrying on and ready to faint, he summoned all his energies for one last effort—and managed to stagger across the line just as the sun was sinking. But as he crossed the line he saw a cruel, cynical smile on the face of the stranger who had promised him the land. Just as he crossed the line—the master and possessor, he thought, of 15 square miles of rich land—the youth fell dead upon the ground which he had coveted.

The stranger then said to the servant, "I have offered him all the land he could cover. Now you see what that is: 6 feet long by 2 feet wide; and I thought he would like to have the land close to his father's grave, rather than to have it anywhere else." With that the stranger, who was Death, vanished, saying as he did, "I have kept my pledge."

---

[1] Scripture references marked *The Living Bible, Paraphrased,* or TLB in parentheses are from *The Living Bible, Paraphrased* (Wheaton: Tyndale House Publishers, 1971) and are used by permission.

[2] B. H. Carroll, *Pastoral Epistles of Paul, 1 and 2 Peter, Jude, 1, 2, and 3 John,* Vol. XVI: *An Interpretation of the English Bible* (Old Tappan, N.J.: Fleming H. Revell Co., 1942), p. 331.

[3] *Ibid.,* pp. 331-32.

6
HOW DO SUCCESS BOOKS RELATE TO THE BIBLE?

Couldest thou in vision see
  Thyself the man God meant,
Thou nevermore couldst be
  The man thou art—content.
                              —A. H. Strong

The best book of success principles ever printed
is the Bible.

Leonard Ravenhill shared a story I have since captioned, "The Parable of the Contented Frog." Some scientists took a frog and dropped him in hot water. The frog hopped out—fast! They dropped him in a second time. Same result. Then they dropped him in a vat of cold water and he relaxed.

What the frog did not know was that the vat of cold water had a fire beneath it. While the frog relaxed the water was heated ever so gradually. The frog sat there, the temperature of the water rose slowly, and before long the frog had been boiled to death.

Isn't that a parable all of us need to hear? We don't know how it is in the frog world, but in our world, it fits to a T. Mediocrity is the fire. Man, represented by the frog, sits and relaxes until his mediocre ways destroy him. Let him stay content without goals and motivations just so long, and one day he will no longer care to move.

A Test and Some Logic

In the twentieth century, some books have been written which might, in a general way, be designated as "success books." In the average city library, several of these can be found, and in some cases, there are a number of them. Basically, these are "How To" books which tell us how we can be successful.

What should a Christian do in this area of his reading? Should he run from them, or run to them? What kind of eye of discernment is needed? How do success books in general relate to the Bible? Is there a conflict?

How about a quiz? This one has only one question. If the statement is true, circle the T. If false, circle the F.

T   F   1.   Truth cannot conflict with truth.

That question is not as easy as it looks, is it? But you guessed right if you circled the T. There is just no way truth from one source can conflict with truth from another one. When there is conflict, only one of the ideas is 100 percent true. Deciding which ideas are totally true is not always an easy decision, but truth is truth, and two truths should not conflict.

Let's approach from another direction. This time let's use logic.

1. Truth cannot conflict with truth.

2. Truth is one area cannot conflict with truth in another area.

3. Truth in one area should therefore complement truth in another area.

To word it another way . . .

1. Truth cannot conflict with truth.

2. Truth in the area of success principles cannot conflict with truth in the Bible.

3. Truth in the area of success principles should therefore complement truth in the Bible (and vice versa).

Whatever real truth there may be in a success book, and whatever real truth there may be in the Bible (I believe it to be completely true), logic suggests there should definitely not be a conflict. The diagram around which this book centers indicates there are conflicts apparent between the two as it now stands. If all the fallacies could be found and removed, success books and the Bible should wonderfully complement one another.

Credit Where Credit Is Due

Many Christians are indebted to success books. Permit a word of personal testimony. This book would never have been written had it not been for some "How-to-Do-It" books I stumbled upon a few years ago. What are some of the ways I am indebeted to success books? Here are a few of the benefits I gained:

1. Gave me a good case of dissatisfaction with myself.
2. Gave me a good case of hunger for achievement.
3. Made me apologize to the Lord that people in the secular world would pay the price of dedication and achievement, and I, in spite of being in the biggest business in the world, would not.
4. Gave me an incredible desire to know how all this related to God's Word.
5. Gave me a great self-image, which incidentally, soon flopped. And that was, frankly, the best thing that ever happened to me. Because my personally instilled and constantly motivated self-image did not work all the time, I suspicioned others had met failure here too. I began to wonder—do you suppose the Bible has something even better to offer?

Success books made this contented frog begin thinking about how to get out of the pond of mediocrity. If you're satisfied with your rut-of-routineness, okay. If you even want to blame your lack of motivation and your lack of goal-setting on the Lord, go ahead. Since most everyone does, it is doubtful one more is going to upset the eternal applecart much more. But if you are tired of blaming God and would like to do something about it, I can recommend you try a success book or two. At least you won't enjoy sitting in the pond of do-nothingness nearly as much. Some of the illustrations of how men dedicate themselves to a goal bring down severe strokes of judgment upon the heads of routine do-nothing Christians.

Fallacies to Watch For

As with any book, the reader of a success book should pray for the wisdom of discernment as he reads. In some books, certainly not all, the reader may quickly spot some of the fallacies listed below.

1. A few of the books only introduce God somewhere after page 300, if at all. Others are more generous and mention his name every 75 pages. The implication, of course, is that God doesn't have very much to do with success, or know very much about it.

2. Some of the books deal with only one side of life—the materialistic. It is possible to have it made materialistically and yet be a total flop in life. The very ones who climb the highest may suddenly see failure staring them in the face. What does one do if his personal empire comes crashing down? Or, the materialistically successful man may just feel miserable in his success! Or, his home may fall apart. Or, his drive to get ahead may give him an ulcer, or a heart attack. Is that success?

3. Some of the books suggest that every man, regardless of his manner of living, is in God's image, and God is anxious to help him succeed. Remember the discussion in chapters 3 and 4? The moral likeness to God has been corrupted by sin. It is only the personality side of the image which is still intact.

4. The source of confidence may differ. The Bible suggests that the believer is to have no confidence in the flesh. He is not to seek more self-confidence, but Christ-confidence. Self seems to disappoint all of us sooner or later, and if that's the only basis for confidence, there may be a shattering of personality.

7
HOW CAN I DEFINE SUCCESS?

Success is much more than a matter of achieving
the right things; it is also a matter of being the
right person.

We must have something to hold up for our young,
as our parents did for us, and say, "This is success,
child. Go after it!"
—Howard Whitman

As we approached the banks of the Schuylkill River in
Philadelphia, the cab driver asked if I had ever seen a car-
crushing machine. "You're about to see your first one then."
He continued, "In a few minutes I am going to show you
entire automobile bodies rolling along in assembly line fashion
on a giant conveyor belt. They will go into a giant car-crushing
machine that cost several million dollars. It takes sixty seconds
to grind a car to bits."

When I saw the instant-crusher, I reflected on the fact that
the desire for achievement grinds up lives nearly that fast.
When the average Joe tries to be successful, he chooses one
of two approaches. Either his method of achieving what he
calls success grinds him to powder; or, his method of achieving
what he calls success grinds to powder the lives of all those
around him. Anytime success is a life crusher, there is something drastically wrong with the definition.

Well, that ought to be easy to get around. Go to the library,
pick up a good book on success, memorize the definition, and
have a go at it. That's what I thought!

I found out it must be easier to put "Success" in the title
of a book than it is to define it (maybe that makes it sell
better). I went to the library, started looking in books which
claimed to be "How To Do It" books on success, and of the

39

first six I picked up, no one even attempted to define it. No wonder lives are getting crushed in the success machine!

Somewhere we better change course. More has been written about it than ever before, but more people know less about it than in any preceding generation.

Allow me to illustrate. An insurance man and I were having lunch together. He was telling me that one of the big areas of his work was selling policies to medical doctors. In the course of the conversation he shared a comment which evoked considerable concern.

"A psychiatrist shared with me that of all the counseling cases he handles, at least one third of them are young people. This is a drastic change from five years ago. But now this is the picture of nearly every day's case load."

Other psychiatrists whom my insurance friend later quizzed all agreed their pattern of cases was no different! After that conversation I began to take note of hospitals where I visited. Invariably I am astounded by the percentage of youth needing help. When I mentioned this at a meeting of ministers, one of the clergymen said he walked onto the psychiatric floor of a large metropolitan hospital and there were so many he thought they were having a youth convention!

Times may be better than ever before, but we can't stand much more of this kind of success!

The hero of a modern novel is in a Paris bar after the Wall Street debacle of 1929. The bartender asks him, "Did you lose a lot in the crash?" He answers, "I lost everything I really wanted in the boom!"

What Success Is Not

A simple little tract entitled "Is This Success?" bears oft repeating. "In 1923 a group of the world's most successful financiers met at the _____ Hotel in Chicago.

"Collectively, these tycoons controlled more wealth than there was in the United States Treasury, and for years newspapers and magazines printed their success stories and urged young people to follow their examples. Here is the rest of the story:

> Charles Schwab—the president of the largest independent steel company—lived on borrowed money the last five years of his life and died penniless.
>
> Richard Whitney—the president of the New York Stock Exchange—served time in Sing Sing.
>
> Albert Fall—the member of the President's Cabinet—was pardoned from prison so he could die at home.
>
> Jesse Livermore—the greatest bear in Wall Street—committed suicide.
>
> Leon Fraser—the president of the Bank of International Settlement—committed suicide.
>
> Ivar Krueger—the head of the world's greatest monopoly—committed suicide."

Someone needs to stop and remind us again—making a living is but the means; life itself is the goal!

In 1961 a Southern businessman addressed 5,000 pastors in St. Louis. The story he shared was tough to tell.

> When I returned to _____ following World War II, five of my closest friends were five of my town's leading business and professional men.
>
> I was with them constantly because we drank and drinking is great for compatible companions. These men had it all made.
>
> One of them was the head of a large flour mill establishment in my state, just one jump from the top bracket in the home office.
>
> Another was the regional head of the largest merchandising establishment in the world.
>
> A third was the head of the largest brick plant in the state.
>
> A fourth was a former Chief Justice of the Supreme Court of our state who returned after the war to practice private law.
>
> The fifth was the president of a bank where I had served.
>
> At this very hour, only one of these men survive. Three are in suicide graves and one died in a mental institution. The lone survivor is living in retirement from a serious physical disability in the very noonday of his life. Were it not for the grace of God, I shudder to think where I would be.

It may be just as important to define what success is not as to define what it is.

Success is not material satisfaction. "For what shall it profit a man if he shall gain the whole world, and lose his own soul" (Mark 8:36).

Success is not selfishness. When an individual sets goals for himself, he must make certain his goals are not self-centered. There is no quicker way for God to withdraw his blessing.

Success is not life without problems. "In the world ye shall have tribulation" (John 16:33).

Success is not ego-mania. Paul wrote to the Galatians, "for if a man thinks himself to be something when he is nothing, he deceives himself" (Gal. 6:3). Some Christians have black-listed any thought of success because of mistakenly relating it to egomania.

Success is not self-confidence. Confidence is to be centered on someone else. "I can do all things through Christ which strengtheneth me" (Phil. 4:13). Jack Hyles has wisely noted, "Many a Christian has withstood the onslaught and attacks of the Devil on all sides only to find himself defeated by self-confidence because of his past victories."

Success is not climbing the organizational ladder by walking roughshod over others. One man Jesus attempted to heal from his blindness was asked whether he could see. He replied, "I see men as trees walking." Jesus knew then that this man was only half healed (still 50 percent sick) and he touched him again and healed him completely. It's a sick man who sees others as no more than trees.

Success is not pleasing everybody. Try to please everybody, and no one will like you because of your vacillating. "Woe unto you, when all men speak well of you" (Luke 6:26).

Success is not being a carbon copy. In the music school of the world's largest seminary (Southwestern Baptist at Fort Worth) they humorously relate the years when most of the music ministers trained there led with three fingers. That's the way the teacher\did it—he had lost two of his in an accident!

The Christian can rejoice, "God does not expect me to be a carbon-copy of anyone!"

Keith Miller, in *A Second Touch*, excitedly exclaims, "What a relief! I saw that I had always been living a life like a suit two sizes too large, sort of hoping I would grow into it. . . . I had never felt at home in my own skin. . . . But now I was discovering that I could just be me, for Christ's sake."

Getting God in the Definition

As you formulate your definition of success, ask, "Is God in it?" God is not about to be catalogued out of the success business. Yet many want God to help them "succeed" just so they can quickly phase him out.

That happens even in the spiritual business. One uses his "spirituality" to get self-pity, another uses it to make himself the center of attention, and another uses it to act crazy so everybody will notice what he can do. In the name of spirituality!

A right definition of success is important from two sides— from the side of having God in it, and from the side of having achievement in it. Defining success without having God in the definition leaves man without the blessing of God upon his life. Yet having God in the life and still not achieving is adding insult to the Infinite.

God knows
>   More about success than man does
>   More about man's needs than man does
>   More about goal-setting than man does
>   More about inner confidence than man does
>   More about power than man does, and
>   More about planning life than man does.

Since God knows all those things and provides the very route to our success, isn't it incredible that we would leave him out of our plans?

What Is Success?

Secular man calls it "the prosperous termination of any enterprise."

The dictionary calls it "the satisfactory accomplishment of a goal sought for."

Wayne Dehoney has conducted several conferences on "Personal Dynamics." In these he has discussed many aspects of success. He defines success as "the progressive realization of a person's worthwhile predetermined goals." He says they must be progressive—with man always moving toward them and always setting more; they must be worthwhile; and they must be predetermined—involving the setting of short-range goals and long-range goals.

Before centering in on one precise definition, some closely related thoughts might help.

Success involves being right with God.

Success involves being able to accept yourself.

Success involves knowing you're on the winning team.

Success involves winning daily victories.

Success involves getting along with others.

Success involves achieving the maximum that can be achieved with what God has given you.

To get a successful definition of success, two things must be considered: (1) the individual himself, and (2) the individual's goals.

Success involves the continued achievement of being the person God wants me to be, and the continued achievement of established goals which God helps me set. Continued—my achievement must go on. It is a daily process, an hourly process, or maybe better—a moment by moment process. It is achievement—reaching for, and accomplishing what I reached for. It concerns my person—it is not something out there, it first concerns something within me. It relates to goals—something that keeps me stretching to become more of what he would have me be. It is always related to God—my person must be, my goals must be. And it is connected with what God wants—with that in mind neither my person nor my goals will miss the mark.

Now ask, Am I being successful? Am I continually being the person God wants me to be? Am I continually achieving the goals God helps me set?

Wise was the man who remarked, "We judge ourselves by what we plan to do. Others judge us by what we have done." We might add, "God also judges us by what we have done, rather than by what we plan to do."

Reviewing—success is the continuing achievement of being the person God wants me to be, and the continuing achievement of established goals God helps me set.

Have a go at it!

8
HOW IS A CHRISTIAN SUPPOSED TO FEEL?

Doctors, and especially those who treat people
suffering from nerves, are realizing more and more
that just as you must keep the laws of health if
you want a healthy body, so there are certain laws
of the spirit you must keep if you want a healthy
mind, peace and inward happiness.
—Gordon Powell

Be of good cheer.
—Jesus Christ

"All right," the skeptic asks, "suppose I revise my definition
of success so that I include both God and goals? What is that
supposed to mean? How would I feel? How is a Christian
supposed to feel? If I committed my way totally to the Lord,
what would happen? What could I expect? I'm sure not interested in heading down Depression Street. Does the Bible tell
how a committed Christian should feel?

Not really. The Bible doesn't say a great deal about feeling.
But what some do not realize is that the Bible indirectly shares
an abundance of thought as well as notable examples on the
subject.

While the manuscript for this book was in the early stages,
I sensed a problem in a church member's life, and felt im-
pressed of God to ask him to come by the office for a visit.
I began the conversation.

"I've wondered if something is wrong. I believe the commitment you made recently was very genuine. Yet I've been
watching as you've listened to the visiting minister. Even
though he has given one of the best presentations of the spiritual life I have heard, I've noticed that you no longer smile.
I wanted to share something with you and ask if this might

be your problem."

Then I placed in his hands the material I am about to share with you. He read only a little ways and looked up excitedly. "That's it! I haven't known how to feel. I didn't know whether I was supposed to smile or frown, be excited or sad."

As he later read how a Christian is supposed to feel and how a Christian can arrive at that point, a wonderful sense of relief enlightened his countenance.

If you haven't known how to feel, don't think you are alone in your frustration. That may just be where most of us are. What do you say we wrestle with it a bit?

Take Your Pick

Our suspicions tell us that our feelings should fall in one of three areas. Read closely, and take your pick!

1. That "top-of-the-mountain" feeling: excited, happy, radiant, thrilled.

Advantage: This is what most everyone wants. Sounds great!
Disadvantage: 90 percent of professing Christians would probably admit failure at staying in this category. Most have tried to feel this way, have wanted to feel this way, have read books on how to feel this way and finally in despair have come to say, "For me it just doesn't work." The positive thinking, success-all-the-time feeling has been tried by most, and despair has resulted.

2. That "just-average" feeling: the Christian is supposed to feel high some of the time, low the rest of the time, expect to feel both up-and-down, high-and-low, and that is the Christian life. Someway these are probably going to average out. The spiritual, "Sometimes I'm up, sometimes I'm down, Oh, yes Lord!" expresses this theory best of all.

Advantage: The main advantage is that this sounds just like we would expect life to sound. We felt that way when we were unsaved, and still feel that way since being saved. Most Christians we know seem to feel this way.

Disadvantage: No one is quite content with this. We get tired of being average. There is no advantage to salvation, because we felt this way before we were saved. Does God save a man for the purpose of being in despair half the time?

3. The "Mr. Humility" feeling: Man should be extremely humble. He should be lowly-in-spirit, a "turn-the-other-cheek" fellow who lets others walk on him, and then he is bound to be pleasing Jesus.

Advantage: Some could interpret that Jesus encouraged this idea. At least, Jesus was the most humble man who ever lived. He did speak of "turning the other cheek."

Disadvantage: This is a very difficult way to live. When we do so, we even get proud of our humility. We can lose all confidence, become negative, and besides, how can one so humble ever be motivated to be an achiever? "Why those others climbing up the organization ladder of success will trample me under!" And besides, Jesus drove money changers out of the Temple, too.

Made up your mind as to how a Christian should feel? Good. Now grab a pencil and write your choice of Feeling No. 1, Feeling No. 2, or Feeling No. 3. Now hold it for a moment while we move on.

9
HOW DO FEELINGS RELATE TO FAITH?

I know that when I take time to talk to God and obey the promptings of the Holy Spirit I feel alive and life is joyous and exciting.
—Peter Marshall

Life's frustrations are a mystery or a challenge, depending on whether they are confronted by faith.

One of my friends has a unique thought-provoking method of making people laugh. He never answers a hallway comment as you'd expect. Ask him, "How're you feeling?" and he replies, "Are you a doctor?"

Bertha Smith, missionary to China for many years, is one of the most delightful people I know. She has a radiance about her that is wonderfully contagious. Well into her eighties, this masterful teacher of the Bible is loaded with enthusiastic freshness. To read her book, *Go Home and Tell*, is never to be the same again.

I've never seen Bertha Smith when I thought she was feeling bad. But "How do you feel?" is one question you shouldn't ask her. "I don't know, I haven't felt of myself lately!" is her usual reply. She simply refuses to live by her feelings.

Ask someone else how he feels and you're in for it worse than that. He'll snarl his face, wrinkle his brow, put on the saddest expression and then take the next thirty minutes telling you how!

Feelings are not nearly as important as we have made them out to be. But do they ever control us!

Six Truths That Could Change Your Life
Most of us sense a vacancy and a void replacing the vitality

we long to have. Pick a group of 100 men and 90 of them would express a desire to feel better. All the vitamins in the world cannot permanently solve the crisis because feelings are not based only on the physical.

Do you believe God wants you to have inner excitement, radiance, thrill, and happiness? (please, none of that mushy, fake kind that turns people off). Then the following six truths may be extremely important.

1. God is definitely interested in how you feel.

2. Satan is a past master at making you feel bad.

3. If you believe your feelings, you may be choosing to believe Satan.

4. The Christian life is not based on feelings.

5. You should learn the fine art of living by faith.

6. Living by faith will make you feel a thousand times better than you ever felt worrying about how you feel.

Now to explain. Study carefully the next few paragraphs because failure right at this point is working psychiatrists overtime.

(1) *God is definitely interested in how you feel.* Jesus knew the tensions of the last week in Jerusalem were almost too much for his troubled disciples, and suggested, "Let not your heart be troubled." When the feelings of Mary and Martha were shattered by death, Jesus wept. When a man felt miserable over his past and repented, Jesus promised him a place in paradise. Again he took special time to speak words to those who mourn, to the poor in spirit, and to those who felt persecuted for righteousness' sake.

Of course God is interested in how you feel. "Cast all your care [that includes your burdens, your frustrations, your feelings] upon him, for he careth for you" (1 Pet. 5:7). If he cared about the lilies of the field, doesn't he care about you? If he saw the lepers, the diseased, the woman in adultery, and cared about how these felt, wouldn't he care about how you feel? He is anxious that you "be of good cheer."

(2) *Satan is a past master at making you feel bad.* The

trouble with most of us is that we are as confused about supernatural powers on the matter of feelings as Job's three friends were on the matter of suffering. Job's friends believed all suffering had to come from God and was sent as punishment for wrongdoing. They never stopped to consider there might be another supernatural power.

When people get saved, Satan soon finds a way to at least make sure they don't always feel saved. He doesn't want them to memorize Romans 10:13, John 5:24, and John 1:12, and 1 John 5:12. He just brings depression feelings and sends the darts of depression often enough that the average believer will quit reading his Bible because he feels so bad.

When Christians start getting concerned over other Christians, Satan again makes them feel bad. As long as he can keep us feeling bad he thinks he's found a way that will keep us from getting concerned. You better believe if Satan can bring boils to Job he can bring depression to you!

Live by your feelings, and Satan will cackle with glee! He is the deceiver! He can deceive you into feeling bad when you have a thousand reasons to feel good. He is a liar! He can whisper to you about how bad you feel when you know that two seconds ago you felt great. Satan is a past master at making you feel bad.

(3) *If you believe your feelings, you may be choosing to believe Satan.* For years, in speaking engagements, I have used the little phrase,

> If you feed your faith, your faith will grow.
> If you feed your doubts, your doubts will grow.
> Whichever one you feed will surely grow.

The life of a first year college student is frequently ruined because Satan thrusts a dart of doubt in his direction. So he quits reading his Bible (which feeds his faith), going to church on Sunday (which feeds his faith), memorizing Bible promises (which feeds his faith), and spends countless hours reading the writings of skeptics. Having fed his doubts, he can't understand why his doubts have grown.

Feelings of doubt, feelings of despair, feelings of depression, feelings of guilt over something confessed 20 years ago, feelings of lust, feelings of anger, are put in our mind by the devil. He wants to keep us far away from "Feeling No. 1" as possible.

(4) *The Christian life is not based on feelings.* The greatest Christians I have known were exciting people to be around. They had troubles and problems same as anyone else (God has no exempt status for his people) but theirs didn't seem to matter so much. They were excited, happy, radiant, and thrilled in spite of it.

What's the difference?

They had mastered one secret most of us have not yet discovered. The secret? The Christian life is not based on feelings. The Christian life is based on faith.

Andrew Murray, in an excellent little work for new Christians entitled, *The New Life*, explains,

Between the life of feeling and the life of faith the Christian has to choose every day. Happy is he who, once for all, has made the firm choice and every morning renews the choice not to seek or listen for feeling but only to walk by faith according to the will of God. The faith that keeps itself occupied with the Word, with what God has said and, through the Word, with God himself and Jesus His Son, shall taste the blessedness of a life in God above. Feeling seeks and aims at itself; faith honors God and shall be honored by Him. Faith pleases God and shall receive from Him the witness in the heart of the believer that he is acceptable to God.[1]

The word "faith" is in the New Testament 234 times; the word "believe" is in the New Testament 251 times; (faith and believe are from the same Greek word, the only difference being in the noun or verb ending); yet the word "feel" or "feeling" is only in the New Testament five times and then it is has nothing to do with telling us how to live.

The absence of New Testament usage of the word re-emphasizes that the Christian life is based on our faith, definitely not our feelings.

(5) *You should learn the fine art of living by faith.* Mention the word faith and some only think of something that happened twenty years ago when they put their faith in Christ. They must think the only meaning of faith is fire insurance!

Faith is fantastic, everyday excitement. Without it you're doomed to despair. Viktor Frankl rotted for years in a concentration camp during World War II and later wrote: "The prisoner who had lost faith in the future—his future—was doomed. With his loss of belief in the future, he also lost his spiritual hold; he let himself decline and become subject to mental and physical decay."

WARNING: It is impossible to live by your faith and your feelings at the same time. It is either-or.

As you seek to master the art, review often these words of Andrew Murray. "Therefore let faith always speak against feeling. When feeling says, 'In myself I am sinful, I am dark, I am weak, I am poor, I am sad,' Let faith say, 'In Christ I am holy, I am light, I am strong, I am rich, I am joyful.'" [2]

(6) *Living by faith will make you feel a thousand times better and give you the inner happiness you've always wanted.* If you've tried years of living by feelings, is it asking too much to live by faith? If living by feelings has not brought happiness, is it really a gamble to try believing God's promises? One verse—memorized—Ephesians 3:20—could start you down the new path.

What Does a Christian Do on a Blue Monday?

Relying on faith instead of feeling should not seem strange to the believer. But in case it does, here's one way to get started.

Go back prior to your conversion experience. For years you were hindered by feeling. You thought, perhaps for years, that there would be a strange sensation to experience first. That feeling never did come! So one day, you tried God's way, opened your heart to receive Christ, and said, "Lord, I need you. By faith I open the door of my heart. I now receive you as my Savior and Lord. Forgive my sin. Take control of my life. Make me the kind of person you want me to be." And it happened, didn't it?

Now, on that blue Monday (by the way, blue Mondays frequently come on Fridays) when your feelings want to drag bottom, I hope you'll get to the end of your rope again. You might pray a new desperation prayer that would sound like this: "Lord, I've been miserable today because I've been living by my feelings. I apologize, Lord. I want to thank you today that you say in your Word I am saved, that whosoever would call upon the name of the Lord would be saved. Thank you, Lord, that your Word means that the day I called upon you I was saved. Thank you that you see all my problems as opportunities for you to work miracles of accomplishment. Thank you that you are able to do exceeding abundantly above all I ask or think! Thank you that today is going to be a great day because you are working on my behalf."

Paul said, "For we walk by faith, not by sight."

Try the faith walk very long, and Feeling No. 1 may be just around the corner. It was for Paul, but you'd never dream of the unorthodox way the apostle arrived there.

---

[1] Andrew Murray, *The New Life* (Minneapolis: Bethany Fellowship, Inc., 1967), p. 105. Used by permission.

[2] *Ibid.*, p. 106.

PART THREE:
STARTING DOWN THE SUCCESS-IMAGE TRAIL

10
PAUL'S BUILT-IN SUCCESS IMAGE

I have no trouble wondering if God wants me
to succeed. The cross is proof enough for me.

Our feelings are revealed by our actions.
—John Haggai

Every Christian prefers Feeling No. 1. Every Christian wants that mountain-top feeling, the feeling of excitement! Happiness is to be excited!

Is this a wrong desire? Not at all. When God created man, he made him supremely happy. Man was excited from the first moment he was created! Sin was the factor that made him less than God's best. When man gets right with God, he should be supremely happy and excited about life, regardless of circumstances. Paul was.

Right at the Top

Knowledgeable men consider the apostle Paul the greatest Christian. In his field, Paul became an outstanding success. He was aggressive, motivated, a positive thinker.

A first-century insurance company looking for a supersalesman would have tried to hire Paul after the first interview! They would have envisioned him reaching the million dollar club!

Scholarly F. W. Farrar, writing one of the great classics on the life of the apostle, said years ago:

How little did men recognize his greatness! Here was one to whom no single man that has ever lived, before or since, can furnish a perfect parallel. If we look at him only as a writer, how immensely does he surpass, in his most casual Epistles, the greatest authors, whether Pagan or Christian, of his own and succeeding epochs. If we look at the Christian world, the very greatest worker in each realm of Christian services does but present an inferior aspect of one phase only of Paul's many-sided preeminence.[1]

Later Farrar discussed Paul as a theologian, a preacher, a practical organizer, a missionary, and a reformer who altered the course of history, before concluding, "No saint of God has ever attained the same heights in so many capacities."

Rising Above Circumstances

Whatever Paul's plan may have been (and we shall uncover his marvelous secret in later chapters), Paul definitely found a way to arrive at Feeling No. 1. And Paul did not maintain his daily thrill and excitement because of circumstances but in spite of circumstances.

Paul could
>   rejoice in tribulation
>>   sing in a prison cell
>>>   help a jailer who had flogged him
>>>>   and if that were not enough

he could write several of the world's great books while serving time as a prisoner. Furthermore, the apostle could stand unafraid while addressing some of the wise philosophers of ancient Athens. This man had what it takes.

He was so confident; he believed he could do anything and accomplish anything that God wanted him to do.

The Source and the Accomplishment

Add it up. Confidence, excitement, zeal, inner motivation, positive thinking, accomplishment of goals, and any way you add, the total is the same—SUCCESS.

Since Paul had no books about success or motivation to read, where do you suppose he received his ideas? Here's a starter. He received his ideas from the one who knows more about success and accomplishment than any other—God. From the Holy Spirit of God who dwelt in Paul's life. When the source of a success-image is right, then the accomplishment is right.

Check Philippians 3:12-14 for accomplishment.

Not as though I had already attained, either were already perfect: but I follow after, if that I may apprehend that for which also I am apprehended of Christ Jesus. Brethren, I count not myself to have apprehended: but this one thing I do, forgetting those things which are behind, and reaching forth unto those things which are before, I press toward the mark for the prize of the high calling of God in Christ Jesus.

Not as though I had already attained.—This shows humility, shows he viewed achievement as an ongoing, continuing process.

This one thing I do.—that's goal-setting. He had written it down. He had taken the purposes of his life, narrowed them into one. One can see the big aim of his life, the main drive, the ultimate passion.

Forgetting those things which are behind.—refusal to dwell on the negatives. If looking back could ever ruin someone, Paul was the one. He had persecuted the church, made havoc of God's work, held the coats of those who had stoned Stephen, and been a leader in the first-century hatred movement. Sins and sorrows had to be forgotten, or success would have fled.

Reaching forth to those things which are before.—exciting enthusiasm about opportunities just ahead.

I press.—burning desire.

toward the mark.—discipline, dedication, shows his fixed purpose.

for the prize.—that winning feeling. He believed he couldn't help but be successful if he could continually be the person God wanted him to be and continually achieve the goals God wanted him to achieve.

of the high calling of God.—setting of priorities.

And that's what it takes to produce a real success image.

Characteristics of a Biblical Success Image

Christianity has well remembered some of the sterling characteristics of the apostle Paul. His best known qualities have been cited for centuries.

APPRECIATIVE—"I thank my God upon every remembrance of you" (Phil. 1:3).

CONCERNED—"For I could wish that myself were accursed from Christ for my brethren, my kinsmen according to the flesh" (Rom. 9:3).

CONSIDERATE—"Wherefore, if meat make my brother to offend, I will eat no flesh while the world standeth, lest I make my brother to offend" (1 Cor. 8:13).

HUMBLE—"Unto me, who am less than the least of all saints" (Eph. 3:8).

SERVANTLIKE—"Paul, a servant of Jesus Christ" (Rom. 1:1).

But little is said about the other characteristics which made the man. Other things to be considered include at least fifteen additional personal strengths.

BOLD—"We were bold in our God to speak unto you" (1 Thess. 2:2).

CONFIDENT—"I can do all things through Christ which strengtheneth me" (Phil. 4:13).

COURAGEOUS—"I withstood him [Peter] to the face because he was to be blamed" (Gal. 2:11).

DETERMINED—When stoned and left for dead, he got up and headed for the next town to preach again (see Acts 14:19).

EXCITED—He was persuaded that nothing could ever separate him from the love of God (see Rom. 8:38-39).

FOLLOWER OF FAITH INSTEAD OF FEELINGS—In the midst of a 14-day storm at sea, he exclaimed, "Sirs, be of good cheer: for I believe God" (Acts 27:25).

GOAL-SETTER—After three missionary journeys, he still wanted to go to Rome and later to Spain to carry on his work (Rom. 15:24).

HAPPY—When he looked forward to going to Rome, where he knew he might die, he said, "That I may come unto you with joy by the will of God, and may with you be refreshed" (Rom. 15:32).

MOTIVATOR OF OTHERS—To Philemon he wrote, "Having confidence in thy obedience I wrote unto thee" (Philem. 21).

PERSISTENT—Two years, while a captive of Rome, living in his own house, apparently with guards guarding him all the time, Paul continued "preaching the kingdom of God" (Acts 28:30-31).

POSITIVE THINKER—"If God be for us, who can be against us?" (Rom. 8:31).

RADIANT—"I shall abide and continue with you all for your furtherance and joy of faith; that your rejoicing may be more abundant in Jesus Christ" (Phil. 1:25-26). Twenty-five times in his letters he talks of his joy.

SATISFIED WITH POSSESSIONS—"For I have learned, in whatsoever state I am, therewith to be content" (Phil. 4:11). "For I have all and abound" (v. 18).

THRILLED—"I have fought a good fight, I have finished my course, I have kept the faith: henceforth there is laid up for me a crown" (2 Tim. 4:7-8).

VICTORIOUS—"And the Lord shall deliver me from every evil work, and will preserve me unto his heavenly kingdom" (2 Tim. 4:18).

I know many of those qualities are listed in our modern flurry of success books. And I'm delighted. I just consider it important that we remember these ideas originated with someone else—someone who was wonderfully in charge of giving daily direction to an apostle's life nearly 2,000 years ago.

---

[1] F. W. Farrar, *The Life and Work of St. Paul* (London: Cassell, Petter, Galpin, and Co., n.d.), II, 579.

11
GETTING POSITIVE TOO SOON

There isn't a pessimistic note in the New Testament after the resurrection.
—Andrew Blackwood

Well then, is it the power of positive thinking that is required? . . . While, in general, it is good to be optimistic, that optimism must have some basis in fact to be of any help at all.
—Ray Stedman

Don't draw the wrong conclusion from Paul's life. Someone could surmise, "If I could simply teach myself to master positive thinking, I'll have it made." As if that was all there was to it.

A mountain of material has been written about positive thinking, but legitimate questions still arise. Paul's strength at this point could get most anybody excited, but it also brings out questions. For instance, how does positive thinking relate to negative commands? Is the Bible a positive book of a negative? Are there problems related to positive thinking? Does it always work? How could Paul always be so positive?

Negatives with a Purpose

God's negatives all have a purpose. Every "thou shalt not" is designed to bless the life. The purpose of all God's negatives is positive!

In order to build a positive person, God must teach us to be realistic. There are not just good things in life—there are bad. So there must not just be "do's," but also "don'ts."

When God says "thou shalt not," he is not saying we may not, nor is he saying we cannot, but he is simply saying we must not if we want to lead a positive life. The All-Wise Eye is charting a course.

61

The disciplined distance runner must memorize well his "thou shalt nots." These are not his main concern. His eye must be on the tape! He wants to be the first to cross the finish line! But he trains himself that he must not look at his feet, he must not burn himself out on the first lap, he must not look back every second to see how the other guy is doing! He can best think positively only when the right negatives are an ingrained part of his thinking.

Why are there negatives in the Bible? (1) Because of the reality of sin and the danger of it. (2) To tell the truth in love. (3) To simulate problems.

A simulation expert sat beside me on a flight high over Chicago. Being totally ignorant of his field, I probed a bit. His firm contracted themselves to high schools or technical schools and taught simulation. Students became excited, grade averages rose, near-dropouts took interest.

"Give me a definition of that word," I suggested, with pencil in hand.

"Simulation is a space-age term relatively new in industry in which firms build models of a complete larger system, imitate every possible wrong turn a mechanism can take."

"My company will discuss with you what you want done, we will build an inexpensive model of your expensive machinery, build in every possible malfunction area, and even teach you how to train your students to use it and learn from it.

"This is the only reason the space program has been a success," he continued. "When something goes wrong on one of the space flights, ground control will make the same thing go wrong in their model at the Houston Manned Spaceflight Center, then dictate directions to the men in the spaceship how to correct their problem."

When I had asked my questions of the young company president, and we had discussed my work for awhile, I had a silent moment to reflect on the truths I had learned that day. God seemed to drive my thoughts on simulation toward the Bible.

For the first time I knew why there were so many Bible stories of people with problems. For the first time I could understand God's reasoning in listing the faults of some otherwise great Bible characters. Now I knew why God persisted in "telling it like it is." The Bible has specific help for every problem area man has. Either (1) the problem area is confronted with a direct command or specific principle which applies, or (2) God gives an account of someone who had a similar problem and shares the results.

So today science uses, as one method of teaching, one of the same methods used centuries ago in the writing of God's Word. And, the young simulation expert suggested, it is definitely one of the best teaching methods ever devised.

The Bible: Both Positive and Negative

A spinster was getting up in years, and still she had no boyfriends. One of her friends found her standing beside a well, sobbing her heart out. "Why are you crying?"

"Well, I saw this well and just got to thinking. One day I might get asked for a date. Then I might really like the fellow and we might get engaged. After that we might get married. Then we might buy that house right over there. Then someday we might have children, and they might play out here in this field. One of our kids might come over here to look and he might lean over too far and fall in the well. Boo hoo, Boo hoo, Boo hoo."

She did have a problem, didn't she?

There's a lesson in all that. If negatives were all God gave us to live by, our thinking would indeed be warped. But there's more. The Bible is both positive and negative. It is the perfectly balanced book for a perfectly balanced life. Rightly interpreted and rightly applied, the Word of God will produce a perfectly balanced life. For like life is meant to be, the Bible is

Negative on sin,
Positive on the Savior.

Negative on self-sufficiency,
Positive on Christ sufficiency.
Negative on human strength,
Positive on divine strength.
Negative on harmful habits,
Positive on helpful habits.
Negative on a sin-filled life,
Positive on a Christ-filled life.
Negative on doubt,
Positive on faith.
Negative on short-sightedness,
Positive on vision.

When Paul got his sin problem settled and his relationship right, he became a very positive individual indeed. Relying on the sufficiency of Christ, he was loaded with positive affirmations.

"I can do all things through Christ which strengtheneth me" (Phil. 4:13).

"My God shall supply all your need according to his riches in glory by Christ Jesus" (Phil. 4:19).

"[God] is able to do exceeding abundantly above all that we ask or think" (Eph. 3:20).

"And we know that all things work together for good to them that love God, to them who are the called according to his purpose" (Rom. 8:28).

"If God be for us, who can be against us" (Rom. 8:31).

"For I am persuaded, that neither death, nor life, nor angels, nor principalities, nor powers, nor things present, nor things to come, nor height, nor depth, nor any other creature, shall be able to separate us from the love of God, which is in Christ Jesus our Lord" (Rom. 8:38-39).

The Bible teaches the kind of positive thinking where one so believes in the power of God to accomplish a task, he moves forward in that power and allows God to work through him in the achievement.

The Main Problem in the Positive Thinking Movement

The whole fallacy of the positive thinking movement is not positive thinking. The fallacy is in getting positive too soon. If we do not get our motivation from God, put our "success" under God, we might be in for trouble. It is not enough to simply start a day saying, "I'm going to be positive." God may choose not to add his blessings to our human methodology when the same human methodology phased him out of the planning.

Suppose an unsaved person cons himself into thinking positively about his spiritual condition. Suppose he repeats fifty times a day "I'm going to think positively about my spiritual condition." Or suppose he frequently says to himself, "Every day in every way I'm getting better and better!" Does his positive thinking change his relationship to God? Is he then God's child?

If a carpenter makes a pulpit stand for a church, can it be said that the pulpit is his child? The piece of furniture is his product, not his child. There's a great deal of difference between being one of God's products and one of God's children. As it would be necessary to be born into the family of a carpenter to be the child of a carpenter, so it is necessary to be born into the family of God to be considered God's child and be a recipient of the blessing he has promised to his children. "Ye must be born again."

Positive thinking, based on truth, carries fantastic blessing. Getting positive too soon, on the other hand, can do irreparable damage.

When J. Edwin Orr was speaking in a meeting in the University of Chicago, a young lady's question began a dialogue:

"I don't understand this. If a man believes in Communism, he is a Communist; if he believes in Socialism, he is a Socialist: well, I believe in Christianity—am I not a Christian?"

"Not necessarily so," I replied.

I noticed that she was wearing an engagement ring, so I

asked:

"Could I ask you a personal question?"

"Certainly," she replied.

"Do you believe in marriage?"

"Of course I believe in marriage!" she replied. "I'm engaged to be married."

"Can you give me any good reasons for it?"

"Marriage," she said, "gives a woman a home and a family, a career and social prestige."

Facetiously, I asked the young ladies in the company present how many of them believed in marriage, and they all gigglingly raised their hands—except one determined spinster.

"That's very interesting," said I. "You all say that you believe in marriage as an institution or a philosophy. It so happens that I am a chaplain of the United States Air Force. I am recognized by state government to perform marriages. This young lady says if one believes in Communism, he is a Communist; if one believes in Christianity, he is a Christian; now you all tell me you believe in marriage: allow me to pronounce you married."

That was greeted with hoots of derision.

"What's wrong with that?" I asked.

"Mr. Orr," protested one girl, patiently, "you know that marriage is not a philosophy; marriage is a personal relationship!"

"Exactly," I returned. "And Christianity is not a mere philosophy; to be a Christian is a personal relationship with Jesus Christ, a living Person."

Why Was Paul So Positive?

Paul seemed to never expect defeat, always anticipated blessing. His God was a big God! There was no task too big for God to do!

How can any one man be such a positive thinker? Was he just better than most of us at conjuring up good positive thoughts? Or was there a basis for it? What is the difference?

Positive thinking (the right kind) is based on three essentials: (1) establishing the right relationship with Christ; (2) keeping the relationship right; (3) being filled with the power of God.

Is it any wonder Paul was a positive thinker? Is it any wonder he possessed such a strong success-image? Paul could afford to be a positive thinker because he kept his life constantly measured by those three essentials.

12
MUST I JUST "ACT AS IF?"

> I know that he is far more willing to do things
> for us than we are to ask him. And that is the
> great mystery. Knowing what I do about God's
> power and God's willingness to help, I keep on
> struggling with myself and trying to work things
> out in my own way when he could save me all
> the anxiety and do it better and easier. I believe
> God is made sad at the sight of so many of us
> trying to work things out for ourselves. He longs
> to help us, but we won't let him; we won't ask
> him.
>
> —Peter Marshall

There's a new game on the market, and the crowds are flocking to buy. Whereas psychiatry is a professional skill for treatment of diseases of the mind, the new fad is a do-it-yourself kick.

Spelling-wise, it might best be called Psyche-I-Atry. You don't need a doctor but you practice this on yourself. It's kin to psychiatry in that it invades both the medical and the mental fields.

The object of the game is to psyche yourself.

Find something you can't do, psyche yourself (psyche the I) and act as if you can do it.

Take the thing you're worried about and psyche yourself, act as if it is not real.

If overtaken by guilt, psyche yourself, act as if there is no real basis for your guilt.

Define success however you like, psyche yourself and act as if God is ready to empower you in the achievement regardless of your definition, motive, or goal.

This game has been recommended by some in relation to suffering. at least one religious group took its roots from the psyching of the individual. "Pain isn't real" they said, "but only a figment of the imagination. Clean up the mind, act as if you don't hurt, and you won't."

Some play the do-it-yourself game with relation to sin. "Psyche yourself by (1) believing there is no such thing as sin or (2) believing circumstances justified what you did. It's all mental; you've no reason to feel guilty. Throw care to the four winds; loosen your strict standards."

Now the game is on the market in relation to success and achievement.

The Risk Is High

In swimming, I either can or I can't. A thousand times I may tell myself, "I know I can swim." If I psyche myself, if I act as if I can when I can't, and jump into the deep water anyway, I may drown.

In war, I can rush the enemy who outnumbers me 10 to 1, and all the while be acting as if I can whip them all, but the odds are real good that I'll soon be dead.

In sickness, I can psyche myself and act as if I don't hurt and I may escape 30 percent of the time, but the other 70 percent will scar or kill.

In sin, I can choose to ignore the reality of it in my life, but much of my joy is lost and I shortcircuit hundreds of blessings in the power area.

In success and achievement, I can psyche myself into emphasizing how much I can accomplish (watch that big "I"). Years hence the realization will come that I have not achieved half of what I could have achieved if God had been directing my life.

It scarcely seems worthwhile to risk your life and your career just because someone said *acting as if* it would work wonders for you. Maybe they forgot to mention that it only works in some things and then it only works some of the time.

Something Better Than Acting

The human body, it has been estimated, may have as many

as ten million nerves. Ten million little nerves to get frustrated. Ten million little nerves with frazzled edges looking for a better way than acting. Ten million little nerves stand pleading for an honest way out of frustration.

Maxwell Maltz suggests that in the business of feeding information into the brain that honesty is the only policy. "The unhappy, failure-type personality cannot develop a new self-image by pure will power, or by arbitrarily deciding to. . . . You cannot merely imagine a new self-image, unless you feel that it is based upon truth." [1] Hence it is imperative we search for a more lasting way than that of psyching ourselves.

Three Basic Laws

Three laws must be understood before we can be assured of success: the law of self-effort, the law of reversed effort, and the law of divine effort.

Law of self-effort.—To win a battle against another power, self must be stronger than that other power. If an individual is to be successful as he battles Satan and temptation, then that individual must be stronger than Satan. Otherwise, he cannot hope to win.

Satan knows how to defeat every one who fights with self-effort. He knows by every weakness, and can at any moment hit me at my weakest point. I am simply not stronger than he is. Analyze the following conversation—(read it in Luke 22:31). (This is a personal paraphrase.)

Jesus: "Simon, Satan is after you, really after you" (v. 31).

Simon: "Don't worry about me, I am ready" (v. 33).

Jesus: "If the way you're going to fight him is through self-effort, the big 'I,' then the outcome is already known. You will soon deny me three times" (v. 34).

Yet self-effort is the way every unsaved person fights the battles of life (only way he can) and the method used by 75 percent of Christians. The longer this method is used, the more likely the next law will come into play.

Law of reversed effort.—If we try too hard not to do something, we will finally do it because we will have impressed it so indelibly upon our minds. Robert Thouless in his book about the psychology of religion discusses this law.

Suppose that you have been told to walk along a plank lying on the floor of the room in which you are at present sitting, without stepping off on either side. You would have very little emotion about the possibility of your failure, and you would accomplish the task quite easily. Now suppose that you have been told that you must walk along something equally rigid and of the same width at a height of several hundreds of feet above the ground. You will almost certainly fall off. What has happened is that your horror of falling off has made the spontaneous autosuggestion of the fall so strong that you have not been able to prevent your mind from realizing it. You will also find, under these conditions, that the harder you try to prevent yourself from falling off, the more certainly you will do so.[2]

James Jauncey adds, "Suppose a young man is troubled with impure thoughts which he finds almost impossible to drive from his mind. The more he struggles, the more involved he becomes. Even prayer does not seem to help. What he is doing is making the problem worse by focusing his mind upon it." [3]

Robert Thouless relates how the plank can be walked.

Your only chance of performing the task successfully is to adopt a method which reduces to a minimum both your fear of the fall and your voluntary effort to keep on the plank; in other words, you must think neither about the height nor about the effort necessary to keep on the plank, but only about getting to the other end.[4]

We are dreadfully slow to learn that the law of divine effort is our only real solution. Simply stated, this law suggests that God is the strongest power there is and divine effort can meet any need or master any situation.

Oswald Chambers, in his excellent book, *My Utmost for His Highest,* must have been thinking about this law.

A river is victoriously persistent, it overcomes all barriers. For a while it goes steadily on its course, then it comes to an obstacle and for a while it is baulked, but it soon makes a pathway round the obstacle. Or a river will drop out of sight for miles, and presently emerge again broader and grander than ever. You can see God using some lives, but into your life an obstacle has come and you do not seem to be of any use. Keep paying attention to the Source, and God will either take you round the obstacle or remove it. The river of the Spirit of God overcomes all obstacles. Never get your eyes on the obstacle or the difficulty. The obstacle is a matter of indifference to the river which will flow steadily through you if you remember to keep right at the Source. Never allow anything to come between yourself and Jesus Christ, no emotion, or experience: nothing must keep you from the one great sovereign Source.[5]

Divine effort, when applied, stops all possibility of failure due to overworked self-effort. Many a Christian has become neurotic by attempting to master self-effort and failing to zero in on Divine effort.

The Bible does not just say, "Resist the devil, and he will flee from you," yet that's the way many people quote it. That would simply be self-effort at its futile best. It would be far better to memorize the entire verse: "Submit yourselves therefore to God. Resist the devil, and he will flee from you" (Jas. 4:7). Submission, turning the problem over to him, enables divine effort to be applied, and Satan knows to flee from that. Satan knows when he has met his match. When he finds a person who turns him over to the Lord, Satan knows he will be defeated.

Anxious that we move ahead to victory God inspired others to teach us this same law of divine effort.

Paul: "Put on the whole armour of God, that ye may be able to stand against the wiles of the Devil" (Eph. 6:11).

Isaiah: "Even the youths shall faint and be weary, and the young men shall utterly fall: but they that wait upon the Lord shall renew their strength; they shall mount up with wings as eagles; they shall run, and not be weary; and they shall walk, and not faint" (Isa. 40:30-31).

John: "Greater is he that is in you, than he that is in the

world" (1 John 4:4). Remember, Satan is the prince of this world.

Self-effort is not sufficient to fight the biggest battle of all—the battle of life. At best self-effort will sooner or later fail you (Satan will see to that); at worst, self-effort will become reversed effort. Blessed is the man who discovers and applies divine effort.

Honesty demands that I admit there are some things I cannot do, some battles I cannot win, some goals I cannot achieve. I can either act as if, or seek an effort greater than mine.

---

[1] Maxwell Maltz, *Psycho-Cybernetics*, p. 25.

[2] Robert Thouless, *An Introduction to the Psychology of Religion* (New York: Cambridge University Press, 1923), p. 52.

[3] James Jauncey, *This Faith We Live By* (Grand Rapids: Zondervan Publishing Co., 1966), pp. 14-15. Used by permission.

[4] *Op. cit.*, pp. 52-53.

[5] Oswald Chambers, *My Utmost for His Highest* (New York: Dodd, Mead, and Co., 1963), p. 250.

PART FOUR:
DISCOVERING THE SECRET

13
CHRISTIANITY IS A RELATIONSHIP

When I became a Christian, Jesus Christ came
to live in my heart in the person of his Holy Spirit.
Real Christianity is really Christ-in-you-ity.
—John Hunter

We are not saved to go to heaven. If so, why didn't
we go to heaven right then? Heaven is a by-
product. We were saved to tell others and to let
Jesus Christ live in us.
—Jimmy Draper

One reason the average man never dreams of relating success
and the spiritual is that his basic understanding of Christianity
is wrong. When he defines Christianity correctly, he will come
to value his spiritual life more than ever before. He will even
see it as the secret to a successful life.

If you were assigned the task of defining Christianity in
a sentence or two, how would you go about it?

A pastor friend has been asked to write a booklet for nation-
wide distribution on the meaning of Christianity.

"Bill," he related, "my problem is that I don't know how
to begin. I'm to write for the new believer, and the assignment
is to say it simply, so a person can understand it regardless
of background."

"Have you considered that Christianity can be defined in
one word?" I asked. "One word?" he queried. "What would
that be?"

The word, of course, is relationship. Christianity is vastly
different from all religious systems, set apart as totally unique,
for Christianity is a relationship—a relationship between two
people. One is you, and the other is Jesus Christ.

My friend seemed to become excited. "that's exactly right!"
he exclaimed. "A man can understand that."

Difficulty Explained

Maybe the problem began because we have wanted to define Christianity by what it does or has rather than what it is.

Check some of the answers you would possibly obtain if you spot-checked with a man-on-the-street interview.

"Christianity is a set of doctrinal beliefs," the first man might remark. Oh, great, that means nobody can understand it unless he has a number of courses. No, Christianity has doctrinal beliefs, but Christianity is a relationship.

"Christianity is being good to your neighbor," a second man explains. That's good thinking, but not a good definition. certainly no other teacher ever gave such a high concept of neighborliness as did Jesus. "Thou shalt love thy neighbor as thyself." However, being a good neighbor is a fruit of the Christian life, not the root.

"Christianity is love," the third man comments. "God is love," the Bible says, and that's the understatement of the first century. According to Jesus the two great commandments are about love—love to God, and love to your neighbor. "We love because he (God) first loved us." Love gets right at the heart of Christianity. The Christian does love, but that definition would only serve to confuse. The ancient Greeks had three words which twentieth-century man might translate as "love": *eros*—sensual, erotic type of love; *filia*—brotherly love, or the friendship kind; *agape*—the Godlike kind of love. If by definition, Christianity is love, some will never understand because their concept of love is scrambled.

Number 4 says Christianity is just another religion. Not so. Christianity is quite different from all religions. For the purpose of filling out forms it will no doubt be classified as a religion from now until Jesus comes, but this cannot be.

> *Religion:* A group of teachings designed to tell a person how to live, designed by a leader who can furnish no power to enable a follower to live up to the teachings

> *Christianity:* A relationship to a living Person who has

not only provided a group of teachings about how to live, but who indwells his follower so as to provide continual power to live the suggested life
Christianity is not a religion. It is a personal relationship!

The Descriptions of Jesus

Calling Christianity a relationship will explain some of the simple statements of Jesus. "Follow me" (Matt. 16:24) was his way of saying, "Let's start the relationship." Those who received him are said to be sons of God (John 1:12). "Ye must be born again" (John 3:7) also speaks of the initiation of a relationship. Born once, a man is related to his parents in a relationship as close as life itself. Born again, a man is related to Jesus. Born once, man has a nature that soon tends toward sin. Born again, man gains another nature, one that is Godlike. Born once, he is a son of Adam. Born again, he is a son of God. Born once, man is an heir of his earthly parents. Born again, he is an heir of God and a joint-heir with Jesus Christ.

The relationship idea also helps to clarify the statements of Jesus which have been considered difficult to interpret. "He that believeth on me . . . out of his belly shall flow rivers of living water" (John 7:38) simply means that when the relationship is established and the relationship is right, there will be an automatic source of flowing power coming from within the life—his power. "Except ye eat the flesh of the Son of man, and drink his blood, ye have no life in you" (John 6:53) was his way of suggesting that unless we believe, we have existance, but not real abundant life—no relationship, no life. "For whosoever shall do the will of God, the same is my brother, and my sister, and mother" (Mark 3:35) suggests that the one who follows Jesus maintains the closest possible relationship to him, a relationship as close as that of a mother and child.

The Necessity of Surrender

Some wonder why intellectual believers (possessing only

head belief) are not saved. If there is no heart belief (surrender and personal commitment to him as Savior and Lord), there is no relationship. It is possible to have been baptized, confirmed, consecrated, and received into the church and still have no power for life. Only the one who has repented of sin and been born again by personal faith in Jesus Christ can claim to have a personal relationship.

Even devils in hell have an intellectual religion, the Bible says. And that with the right God! "Thou believest that there is one God; thou doest well: the devils also believe, and tremble" (Jas. 2:19). The biting sarcasm of James 2:19 suggests, "You even believe in God [you have head belief]?" Congratulations! You have now advanced to the same stage as the devils in hell!"

But I believe in God.
So do the devils in hell.
I even believe God had a son named Jesus.
So do the devils in hell.
But I even believe Jesus died to save sinners.
So do the devils in hell.
But I know Jesus does save sinners.
So do the devils in hell.
I even know I'm a sinner.
So do the devils in hell.

But there is one place the comparison stops! When a person who intellectually believes, takes one step farther and yields his life to Christ, Christ will initiate a personal relationship with that person. The devils come to a screeching halt at that point—they rebel and tremble.

The Power of the Relationship

"I'm in the ditch," the man pleaded. "Help me!"

"Here is a list of seven steps," the Buddhist said kindly. "If you follow these, you will have a good life."

"I can tell you which direction to face if you want to pray while you're in that ditch," the Muslim commented. "If you want out, pray in the right direction."

Several others walked by and offered suggestions, and the man was all ears. He appreciated the advice, but he was powerless to get out.

Until Jesus came by.

"If you want me to, I will come down to where you are, put my strength into your body, and with my power in you we'll together come out of that ditch!"

Christianity is a personal relationship between two people in which One person provides the power the other needs. Religion cannot provide that power but Christ can.

The Promise of a Continued Relationship

Jesus chose some disciples, related himself personally to each one and they liked that. Until the week came for him to die.

They came unglued. Sensing they were shaken, he calmed them. "Let not your heart be troubled" (John 14:1). "I have been related to you, but it's not all over. I will come again and receive you."

"And if you're wondering what will happen in the meantime—I've provided for that too. I will not leave you comfortless—I will come to you. How? Let me tell you about the Holy Spirit." (see John 14:1-3,16-18).

Through the Holy Spirit, the relationship Jesus had initiated with the disciples would wonderfully continue. They would have with them, wherever they went, the secret to a successful life.

14
THE HOLY SPIRIT: WHO HE IS AND WHAT HE DOES

> You are going to make history with even greater
> success stories than those written about me.
> —Jesus Christ
> (John 14:12, paraphrase)

> Two extremes have developed about the Holy
> Spirit. "If I think of being Spirit-filled," the
> average believer concludes, "I will either (1) lose
> all confidence, or (2) be expected to act crazy."
> As long as Satan can keep him thinking that way,
> he has the man where he wants him—not desiring
> to be filled with God's fullness and not having
> God's power for his everyday practical life.

Time: the last week of the earthly life of Jesus.

Place: Jerusalem

Setting: Jesus, speaking to his disciples, seeks to prepare them for the cross.

Jesus was about to conclude a three-year ministry, the deeds of which would still be shared with thousands of people nineteen centuries later. During these three years the crowds had discovered that Jesus was

Confident

a dreamer

A master motivator

An extraordinary goal-achiever

Filled with the power of God

A personality who drew great crowds

Loaded with love

Yet bold and brave.

His subject matter in this last conversation with his disciples prior to the cross concerns two things: (1) the Holy Spirit, and (2) success.

The success they would achieve would be gigantic. "He that believeth on me, the words that I do shall he do also: and greater works than these shall he do; because I go unto my Father" (John 14:12).

The disciples simply sat amazed, wondering how. Jesus continued, "The Holy Spirit shall dwell with you and shall be in you" (v. 17). Jesus was saying, "You will be programmed for success. I have no doubt you will achieve it."

The person and power of the Holy Spirit was programmed to become a part of every born-again believer's life.

The Third Invasion

Since the days of creation there have been three distinct invasions—three unique ways God has shared his power with the human race.

The first invasion—when
God invaded creation to walk
with the Adams and the Enochs.
    The second invasion—the
    birth of Jesus. God had in-
    vaded history to put his Son
    in Jewish clothes.
        The third invasion—the indwelling Holy
        Spirit. "It
        is expedient that I go away,"
        he had related. "But he [the Holy Spirit]
        shall be with you and in you."

Paul would later describe Invasion No. 3 as a unique mystery: "Even the mystery which hath been hid from ages and from generations, but now is made manifest to his saints: to whom God would make known what is the riches of the glory of this mystery among the Gentiles; which is Christ in you, the hope of glory" (Col. 1:26-27).

What a mystery and what a miracle! Born-again believers would have a unique power within—Christ himself would be dwelling within their lives through the Holy Spirit.

Who Is the Holy Spirit?

He is the key to the relationship.—No key was needed while Jesus was alive. They could see Christ with them, feel his power around them, be assured when he spoke to them, answer questions for them, and lift burdens from them. But if he was not around?

Then they would need him around. "It is expedient [wonderfully necessary] for you that I go away," Jesus said. The purpose of his leaving was so that he, through the Holy Spirit, could be around all the time—with each separate one, in the city of his residence, to provide the exact power needed in each situation. When he would be working in many different locations all at once, they would do greater works, reach more people, achieve more accomplishments in his name than he had done during the short years of his ministry.

He is the source of real power.—The Old Testament prophet had revealed remarkable truth—"Not by might, nor by [human] power, but by my spirit, saith the Lord" (Zech. 4:6). Jesus had reemphasized it to the disciples. "Ye shall receive power, after that the Holy Spirit is come upon you" (Acts 1:8). The book of Acts explodes with the punch of power. The disciples denied it was their power (3:12), but insisted it was the power of the Holy Spirit producing the miracles (4:7-8). Check the source of Stephen's power (6:3,8). Or hear Peter's explanation of why Jesus had power—"God anointed Jesus of Nazareth with the Holy Spirit and with power" (10:38).

The Holy Spirit is also Christ in you!—Jesus promised, "I will come to you" and 8 verses later said, "He shall be with you and in you" (John 14:8, 16-17). The coming One was Jesus, but now Jesus through the Holy Spirit rather than in physical form. He would be another Comforter (Greek, another of exactly the same kind), John 14:16.

Other Bible descriptions of the Divine Motivation Expert are:

"Christ in you" (Col. 1:27).

"If Christ be in you." (Rom. 8:10)

"His Spirit that dwelleth in you" (Rom. 8:11)

"If any man have not the Spirit of Christ" (Rom. 8:9).

"Spirit of him that raised up Jesus from the dead
dwell in you" (Rom. 8:11)

"Christ liveth in me" (Gal. 2:20).

"For to me to live is Christ" (Phil. 1:21).

"Christ, who is our life" (Col. 3:4).

Harold Wildish asks, "Did you hear of the three men who claimed ownership of the same house?"

"I bet they had a fuss over that."

"No, not at all. The first man was the builder of the house. He planned the whole thing and put it up for the sale. The second man was the buyer who now is the owner and then he has rented it to the tenant who now resides there."

"God the Father made it. God the Son with his precious blood redeemed it, bought it at Calvary; God the Holy Spirit has come to reside within." Then Wildish comments, "Surely the God who made, redeemed, and possessed man would be sufficient to make him the victorious Christian he longed to be" (from *The Glorious Secret*, p. 6).

The Work of the Holy Spirit

The Holy Spirit (1) establishes the relationship; (2) enforces the rules; (3) enriches the life; (4) empowers for service.

At the time of salvation the personal relationship is *established*, the Holy Spirit enters, and is "with you" and "in you" (John 14:17). In fact, "If any man have not the Spirit of Christ, he is none of his" (Rom. 8:9).

Enforcing the rules (teaching) is another vital part of the work of the Holy Spirit within. Jesus said, "He [the Holy Spirit] shall teach you [the believer] all things" (John 14:26). Many methods of teaching are used, but one of the more noticeable methods is "chastening" (see Heb. 12:6-7). God chastens or spanks when necessary, but only to teach the believer to be a better child next time. When the teaching is over, the sin confessed, the believer can afford to move on to better things.

Enriching the life is no less important in the Holy Spirit's work. Even as Jesus spoke to the disciples of the Holy Spirit, he promised fantastic peace. There would be no need for them to be troubled nor afraid (John 14:27). Furthermore, the life would be fruitful. Dawson Trotman suggested the Christian is "born to reproduce." Jesus said, "I have chosen you and ordained you, that ye should go and bring forth fruit." But that's not all! After speaking to them about the Holy Spirit, He told them why—"These things have I spoken unto you that . . . your joy might be full" (John 15:11).

Empowering the believer is perhaps the greatest work of all. Every believer has the Holy Spirit (Rom. 8:9) but comparatively few have found the secret of his unusual power for daily living.

But the subject of the Holy Spirit's role in providing power demands a chapter by itself.

15
FILLED WITH GOD'S FULLNESS

The road to success is always under construction.

Being filled with the Spirit is an inside job. If
you insist on an outer experience, then you make
emotions the king.
—Jack R. Taylor

Years ago someone stated, "I used to think a few men had
a monopoly on the power of the Holy Spirit. I have since
learned the Holy Spirit has a monopoly on a few men."

The believer cannot be as successful as God intends, cannot
have the peace, joy and abundant life God desires for him,
unless he comes to understand what it is to "be filled with
the Spirit." The purpose of this chapter is to lead the believer
to enjoy the Spirit-filled or Christ-controlled life.

But first let's analyze three little verbs. Analysis of negative
reactions will hopefully lead toward application of a positive
command, the end result being the achievement of power
within.

Negative Reactions Toward the Holy Spirit

"Ye do always resist the Holy Spirit" (Acts 7:51).

"Quench not the Spirit" (1 Thess. 5:19).

"Grieve not the Holy Spirit" (Eph. 4:30).

Many never discover the joy God desires for them to possess.
Why? Some resist God's Spirit, others quench God's Spirit, and
still others grieve him. What's the difference?

Resisting the Holy Spirit is an act performed by an unsaved
person. When this verb is used, Stephen is speaking to unsaved
people who were resisting (or fighting off) the Spirit of God
as he was convicting their hearts of sin. Even as Stephen shared,
they resisted.

The unsaved person has many ways he can resist the Holy Spirit because there are many ways God calls him. Sometimes God speaks through his goodness (Rom. 2:4); sometimes through a concerned relative or friend (John 1:40-41); sometimes through trouble (Acts 16:25-34); sometimes through a sermon (1 Cor. 1:21); sometimes through a Bible verse (2 Tim. 3:15); and sometimes through a still small voice (1 Kings 19:9-12). And sometimes God uses all of these! When God speaks, regardless of the method he chooses, the unsaved person either receives or resists. If he resists, he never receives the joy God has for him.

Quench not the Spirit is Paul's statement to the Thessalonians, in a letter written shortly after he left the city in A.D. 54. Undoubtedly he was writing to many new Christians. God impelled him to remind them to "quench not the Spirit." Quench means to "extinguish or cool suddenly." Every new believer faces this danger in the first few months of being a Christian. While the conversion experience is still fresh, Satan whispers, "You didn't mean that. That was a moment of emotion. Don't do anything else about it." To fail to obey God's direct commands and to follow God's leadership is to "quench the Spirit." Again, joy flees.

Grieve not the Holy Spirit was the negative used in Ephesians. David Smith, in *Life and Letters of St. Paul,* suggests that the three years Paul spent in Ephesus were from A.D. 53-56. But it was A.D. 62, six years later, when Paul wrote back for the first time. Paul's converts had been saved at least six years!

Grieving speaks of a heretofore close relationship, established over a period of time. We grieve only those we know intimately. We grieve the Holy Spirit because we have walked closely with him in days gone by. Sin grieves the one who cares the most about us.

"Grieving" occurs when we (1) revert from a Christ-controlled life to a self-controlled life, (2) seem content with second best in our choices, and (3) expect God to do little or nothing through us (and give him just that much opportunity!). It is sad indeed when a believer spurns God's love and grieves the Holy Spirit.

The Positive Command for the Believer

"Resist not," "quench not," and "grieve not" share only the negative side. On the positive side, the command is "be filled with the Spirit." "Grieve not the Holy Spirit," Paul commands, and then quickly adds: "Be filled with the Spirit" (Eph. 4:30; 5:18).

The sidetracks which divert our attention from "being filled" are astonishing. Some people would mistakenly have us searching for "the gift of the Holy Spirit." However, the gift of the Spirit is received at the moment of salvation (Acts 2:38). In fact, "If any man have not the Spirit of Christ, he is none of his" (Rom. 8:9). It is in the conversion experience, through the act of faith, that we receive the gift of the Holy Spirit (Gal. 3:13-14). Simply put, we receive the wonderful gift of having him live in our lives to give help, direction, and power.

Others suggest a "Holy Spirit baptism" is needed. True, Jesus had suggested to his disciples they would be "baptized with the Holy Spirit but he added, "not many days hence" (Acts 1:5). On the day of Pentecost his prophecy was fulfilled. They were baptized (immersed or covered with) the power of God's Holy Spirit (Acts 2). After Acts 2, the Bible takes a new turn—a dramatic switch in terminology. And there is a reason—Pentecost, as a day or as a happening, did not need to be repeated. God had immersed his young church with power. God had done exactly what he had wanted and promised to do on that day.

For those who live on this side of Pentecost, there is a new emphasis.

Acts 4:8 "Then Peter, filled with the Holy Spirit"
Acts 4:31 "And they were all filled with the Holy Spirit."
Acts 6:3 "Seven men, full of the Holy Spirit and wisdom"
Acts 6:5 "Stephen, a man full of faith and the Holy Spirit"

Acts 7:55 "He, being full of the Holy Spirit, looked up."
Acts 11:24 "He was a good man and full of the Holy Spirit and faith."
Acts 13:9 "Paul, filled with the Holy Spirit"
The divine imperative is for us to be filled with the Spirit.

Wonderfully Practical

When the Bible commands us to be filled with the Spirit (Eph. 5:18), and when it suggests we be filled with all the fulness of God (3:19), the result is the same. We are simply to be so related to the one within that he is captain and Lord of the life.

He wants not just to be resident but also President.

He wants not just to be living within but to be Lord within.

He desires not just to be Messiah but to be Master.

God is suggesting he knows more about how to run a life than any one of us. He longs that we be filled with his fulness.

Jack Taylor's *Key to Triumphant Living* has been wonderfully helpful to a number of people at this point. An excellent pamphlet is the one by Dr. Bill Bright (Campus Crusade for Christ) entitled, "Have You Made the Wonderful Discovery of the Spirit-filled Life?" Texas Baptists have also produced a very helpful booklet, "How to Have the Spirit-filled Life."

How to Be Filled Each Day

The real issue is, "Can God be trusted?" If he can, we should stake our whole lives on him.

When a life is self-controlled, it possesses only the power that can be generated by self. When a life is Christ-controlled, the unlimited power supply of God is always available.

For Christ to control the life, the believer must daily crown Jesus Lord of the life. The process may be called the three C's.

(1) Confess every known sin and ask his forgiveness, claiming his promise of cleansing in 1 John 1:9.

(2) Crown Jesus Lord of the life by an act of volition and

tell him so. Ask him to show you those places in your life which you have heretofore petitioned off (acting as if you knew more about life than he did).

(3) Claim his fullness according to his promise in 1 John 5:14-15.

It is very important that the three C's become a daily practice. The calm quiet of the prayer closet each morning can lead the believer to experience the abundant joy of the Spirit-filled life. With Jesus crowned Lord of life, the believer moves to face the day with excitement. Not self, but Jesus Christ is now in charge.

Someone could ask, "Does the concept of the Spirit-filled life teach a doctrine of perfection? Not at all. In fact, it teaches exactly the opposite. It teaches the Bible doctrine of imperfection by showing the need to crown Jesus Lord of our lives every day anew.

Reason dictates that a life with Christ in charge (a life filled with the Holy Spirit) could produce a dramatic change in the power to achieve.

Suppose Christ was in charge of your life today and you were confident of that one fact. Results?

(1) You could enjoy living with yourself, and this time do it without the ego-bit. He would be the power behind the life, not you.

(2) You could rejoice more, trusting problems to him. After all, problems belong to the one in charge.

(3) You could expect the power of God as you daily confront tough situations.

(4) You could thrill to bigger goals, knowing he is able to do exceeding abundantly above all that we ask or think (Eph 3:20).

(5) You could meet each temptation with prayer, thanking him that "greater is he that is in you [Jesus Christ] than he that is in the world [Satan]." This would be the same as saying, "Lord, I cannot win this fight, but you can. I am not greater than Satan, but you are. I am trusting you to be my victory."

16
SELF-IMAGE; CHRIST-IMAGE

Success is expected in God's children (Josh. 1:8), but nowhere does the Bible even hint that self is the power that brings it to pass.

Christianity is a science, a deep science, which tries to do away with the evil or the fall into selfishness by substituting for self the Son of God, which is Christ.

—F. B. Meyer

A college boy sent a telegram home saying, "Mom, have failed everything, Prepare Pop." The boy received this reply the next day: "Pop prepared. Prepare yourself."

There's the toughest battle of all. Most of us have our biggest problem in getting self prepared.

By the way, how do you go about that?

Two Natures

A counselor may suggest, "Get a good appreciation for the kind of person you are—the kind of person God made you."

Analyze that suggestion. Is it possible? If you get such appreciation of yourself, can you maintain it?

(1) You desperately want to appreciate yourself.

(2) You sometimes thoroughly appreciate what you see.

(3) Other times you know you are not what God made you to be—hence you cannot appreciate yourself.

It is important to understand that the believer has two natures. One nature is displeasing to the Lord. The other nature is made in his likeness. The first is the self nature, or fleshly nature. The second is the new nature, the Christlike nature.

When I have unconfessed sins in my life, and have made

no attempt to confess them to Christ, I am allowing the carnal nature to rule. When that nature sits on the throne of my heart, I just simply cannot be satisfied with myself, try as I may. Nor should I be. I have enough inner sensitivity to tell me that however God made me, that's not the way he did it. I've been interfered with!

Rather than admit there's a self I can't stand, I go into the business of excusing myself—as if God didn't know me better than that. A Tulsa newspaper recently carried a classic example.

Judge Gets Verdict by Mail

WICHITA, KAN. (AP)—The blizzard this week forced everyone to cope with unusual circumstances.

One Wichita man was scheduled to appear in Municipal Court Tuesday with a speeding charge. The court was closed because of the heavy snow, and the following letter arrived in the court clerk's office Friday:

"I was scheduled to be in court February 23, 1971, at 12:15 P.M. concerning a traffic ticket. Well, I was there as scheduled. And to my surprise I was the only one there. No one called and told me that court would be closed.

"After going through the snow to be there on time, I decided to go ahead with the hearing as scheduled, which meant that I had to be the accuser (the patrolman who gave me the citation) and I had to be the accused and also the judge.

"The citation was for going 46 miles per hour in a 35 mile per hour zone. I had the speed alert on my car set on 44 miles per hour. As the accuser I felt that I was going over 35 miles per hour, but as the accused I knew that I was not going 46 miles per hour and as the judge, and being the understanding man that I am, I decided to throw it out of court this time, but it had better not happen again."

In confession of sin, two extremes are possible. Guard against these:

1. *Act as if there is little or nothing to confess.* Unconfessed sin leads to a guilt hangup.

2. *Morbid introspection.*—This person sees more than God sees.

The psalmist had a simple but excellent plan. On his knees in prayer, he asked God to reveal things to him—"Search me, O God, and know my heart: try me, and know my thoughts: and see if there be any wicked way in me" (Ps. 139:23). If you ask him to reveal things in you that are displeasing to him, you can bet he will!

Fallacy of the Self-controlled Man

Sit down and brace yourself. You may need to think on this one a while. But if the Bible is true, then there is no such thing as a totally self-controlled man.

Not that man doesn't want to be, try to be, and hope to be. But it so works out he doesn't get to be. There's someone out to make certain man doesn't control himself.

1. Satan is out to ruin our lives by usurping control (1 Pet. 5:8).

2. Satan does not expect to fail. He has never failed completely except on one person—Jesus Christ (Heb. 4:15).

3. Every other person who has ever lived has done Satan's bidding (sin) sometime or other (Rom. 3:10,23).

4. Since Satan has proved himself stronger than all of us, we can correctly assume he is stronger than self.

5. Therefore no one is completely self-controlled, for at times Satan is in control, persuading us to disobey God.

That trickster! Before a person sins, he is heard to say—"I can do whatever I want to do!" Afterward comes the remorseful—"I don't know why I did that—that wasn't what I wanted!" Instead of self-control, that's Satan-control! The one who starts out as a "I want to run my own life" person invariably winds up as a "Something is ruining my life" person. That's how powerful Satan is.

Sin is not s-i-n. It is s-I-n. Sin is the big "I"—the big drive of self to control the life. The big "I" sees to it there's not much time for God.

Inferiority Complex?

"But I don't like all this new talk I am hearing about 'self.' There's nothing wrong with self, is there? If I can't have a good self-image, won't I have a terrible inferiority complex?"

Two areas are of immediate concern—(1) Does man have trouble with himself? (2) Will a Christ-controlled life rather than a self-controlled life lead to an inferiority complex?

Does Man Have Trouble with Himself?

Dwight L. Moody, the famed evangelist, admitted, "I have more trouble with myself than any other man I've ever met."

Bible characters seem to honestly admit they had trouble with themselves. And they were great men!

Job   "Then Job answered the Lord and said, "Behold I am vile" (Job 40:4).

David   "For I acknowledge my transgressions, and my sin is ever before me" (Ps. 51:3).

Ezra   "I blush to lift my face to thee, my God; for our iniquities are increased over our head" (Ezra 9:6).

Isaiah "Woe is me! for I am undone; because I am a man of unclean lips, and I dwell in the midst of a people of unclean lips" (Isa. 6:5).

Paul   "Christ Jesus came into the world to save sinners, of whom I am chief" (1 Tim. 1:15).

If I have trouble with self, and self sits in the control tower, then I have trouble in the control room!

Jesus startled the first-century world by telling men to deny themselves. "If any man will come after me, let him deny himself, and take up his cross, and follow me" (Matt. 16:24).

Paul recognized that when self was in charge there would be some wrong affections and lusts. He suggested we crucify the flesh. "They that are Christ's have crucified the flesh with the affections and lusts" (Gal. 5:24). Crucifixion is also his descriptive term in Galatians 2:20; 6:14; and Romans 6:6,11.

When Paul mentioned being "crucified with Christ," he

was giving you a glance into his prayer closet. He had dealt
with self (or the old nature) rather harshly. "Come on down
off that throne!" he must have said. "Paul is not about to
be a self-controlled man. I tried that before. The control tower
in this life belongs to Jesus. You (the old nature) can just go
bury yourself. You're finished, through, out of it. Jesus is in
charge of Paul's life from now on."

"Okay, suppose I buy that, and suppose in my prayer closet
I daily enthrone Christ as Lord of my life. Suppose I am no
longer self-controlled, but Christ-controlled. Won't I feel inferior?"

Will Christ-Control Lead to an Inferiority Complex?

Two things desperately need to be said at this point. If
the first idea startles, the second with soothe. If the first
troubles, hopefully the second will thrill.

1. The believer is inferior in some areas. He knows he is
inferior to the Lord. This is derived from simple honesty. Does
it bother him—no! He is thrilled to know there is Someone
who has strength he doesn't. He knows he is inferior to the
devil. His logic convinced him of this. Having yielded to wrong
thoughts or attitudes before, he knows it could happen again.
He knows he is inferior at living the Christian life. Since only
one has ever lived the Christian life like it should be lived,
the believer realizes his lack of ability in this area.

When Christ is crowned Lord of the life, the believer should
refuse to feel inferior in some areas. He should refuse to feel
inferior to the devil if Christ is on the throne of his life. Christ,
who is in charge of his life, is greater than the devil. First
John 4:4 says, "Greater is he that is in you than he that is
in the world" (and that includes the Prince of the world).
He should refuse to feel inferior to problems if he is rightly
related to Christ. Christ, who is in control now, is greater
than those problems. He should refuse to feel inferior to anxieties if he is rightly related to Christ. The Christ who lives
within is greater than those anxieties, or the thing that brought

on the anxieties.

Approach the matter from another direction. The believer is a son of God, a child of the King. Should a child of the King feel inferior? Yes, he should feel inferior to the King. Also, he may rightly feel inferior if he is separated from the power of the King and meets a power stronger than he is.

But those are the only times a child of the King should feel inferior. For any time the power of the King is with him, it would be foolish to have an inferiority complex.

A right relationship each day is vital, since Christ is the power line who supplies the confidence needed for everyday achievement.

Success-Image, Yes; Self-Image, No

So now we come to some important terminology. Should the believer have a success-image? The answer is yes. Remember Paul's built-in success image (Chap. 10)?

However, to say that Paul possessed a great self-image would be misleading. Success-image, yes; but self-image, no.

In chapter 7 success was defined. Success is the continuing achievement of being the person GOD wants me to be and the continuing achievement of established goals God helps me set.

Self-image could be construed to imply that the secret to success is based on self—self's ability to be, and self's ability to do. The Bible would nix that.

Success-image relates to excitement within: (1) Determination that in his power I can be the person God wants me to be; (2) belief that in his power I can achieve the goals he helps me set.

Toward a Success-Image

Those who desire to move toward a success-image should remember that Paul got his success-image only because he sought a Christ-image.

Seeking to please Christ brought all the wheels of the life

into alignment. When his definition was aligned with that of the Lord, and his life was aligned with the wishes of the Lord, and his goals were aligned with those of the Lord, then his success would certainly please the Lord!

Is it any wonder why God chose to bless that life with his power? To possess a failure-image when all those things were brought into alignment would have been an insult to God.

Now it can be said—a success-image is simply a by-product of getting right and staying right with God!

To be a success, it is imperative to seek—

Not more self-control, but more Christ-control.

Not more self-centeredness, but more Christ-centeredness.

Not more self-esteem, but more Christ-esteem.

Not more self-confidence, but more Christ-confidence.

Not more self-power, but more Christ-power.

Not more self-reliance, but more Christ-reliance.

PART FIVE:
MOTIVATED FOR ACTION

17
"IF"—THE BIG HINDRANCE TO MOTIVATION

A man is going nowhere as long as he lives in the realm of the conditional. His vocabulary will be full of words like "if," "provided," "in case," "if so," "unless," "in the event of" until someone may well want to stop and ask, "Sir, is God dead?"

Why do you say, *If* God can use me." Didn't God use a rod, a jaw-bone, five small stones, a handful of oil and a little meal, five barley loaves and two small fishes?

A young preacher, now wonderfully used of God, was having it rough a few years ago. The church he was in was small, nothing exciting was happening, and the thought struck him, "If I could just change churches."

Attending a pastor's conference some months later, he approached the pastor he most respected. "Dr. _____, my church is not going so well, and I don't think I'll ever be able to get those people excited. If you happen to hear of some church in another state which needs a pastor, you might keep me in mind."

Waiting anxiously to hear, "Sure I will, I'll give you a great recommendation," he received the surprise of his life. The highly successful pastor pushed a long finger right toward his face and said, "Let me tell you something, young preacher, and don't you ever forget it. You'll never be happy anywhere until you get happy where you are!"

The young preacher went back to his small, struggling church field, spent a night in prayer on his knees, and dedicated himself to reach the unsaved of that town, and from that moment on God mightily blessed his ministry.

The believer must not allow anything to keep him from

God's intended plan of success. He must at all costs be the person God wants him to be, and achieve the goals God wants him to achieve. God's plan for his life must not be sidestepped, for God's plan alone will bring him maximum happiness. No new geographical location will bring it to pass.

Caution—if anything can keep you from achieving the goals God has for you, it is one word—If.

Twentieth-Century Success-Stoppers

The most prevalent word to prevent us from thinking positively—the most prevalent word to damage our effectiveness in being what God wants us to be and achieving what God wants us to achieve is the word IF.

For a person to claim to be rightly related to the Lord and not allow God to achieve through him is tragic indeed. Yet most of us can readily locate ourselves in the following list:

If I only had time to read my Bible . . .
If I had more power . . .
If I was healthy like he is . . .
If there was something they would ask me to do . . .
If my work didn't make me so tired . . .
If only I had the energy those young people have . . .
If our church wasn't like it is . . .
If I were talented . . .
If those other Christians I know would get on the ball . . .
If my job wasn't so demanding . . .
If my kids would read that Bible and practice it . . .
If I made the money he does . . .
If I could memorize those promises . . .
If I had a better pastor . . .
If God did it like that in our day . . .
If my church had the prospects that other church has . . .
If I didn't live next door to them . . .
If my husband (wife) loved God more . . .
If I could forgive myself . . .

If I didn't have to go to work so early . . .

If they bragged on me like they brag on him . . .

If only I could have lived when Jesus did . . .

If God didn't have it in for me . . .

If I didn't have to live with my past . . .

If my parents could just understand me . . .

If they ever elect me as a deacon . . .

If my boss didn't have it in for Christians . . .

If I had the training and education he had . . .

If I could speak like the preacher speaks . . .

If I had not made that wrong move . . .

If I could have had an easier time growing up . . .

If we ever get to move to a better house . . .

If I had faith like that . . .

If I just knew what to say . . .

If someone would have taught me how to witness when I was young . . .

One common bond unites all those excuses. The blame for nonaction is elsewhere—never where it belongs.

How many of the twentieth-century success-stopper statements have you used?

The Most Destructive Word

"If" is the word of delay. No inner voice need be totally negative. No one needs to tell us we "cannot" do a task. Enough delay will come through slight implication. "Fine, if you can do it," a voice seems to say. Hearing that we don't even attempt.

We are somewhat like the dentist who was bent over working on his patient. The patient in the chair cried, "Here, Doc, you haven't pulled the right tooth!" The dentist replied calmly, "I know it, my good man, but I'm coming to it."

"If" is the word of despair. Delay an action once, and the chances of getting it done diminish. Delay it several times and we may never do it. When God impresses a task upon the mind, and we surrender to some "if," we will be frustrated and in despair.

"If" destroys incentive, wrecks confidence, assassinates character, robs us of God-given dreams, ruins our adventuresome spirit. An unknown author cautioned:

On the plains of hesitation,
Lie the bleached bones of thousands,
Who, on the very threshold of victory,
Sat down to rest,
And while resting, died.

Great Men Not Exempt

One might suspect that great men would be exempt from "if" trouble. Not so. The great servants of God, though plagued with the problem, move beyond it by trusting the Lord's power to be bigger than the problem. (See Eph. 3:20.)

If I were Satan, this is the one word I would seek to lodge in the minds of people more than any other, and my major emphasis would be to place it in the minds of God's sharpest servants. The ones most plagued with "ifs" would be the ones God would otherwise most likely use to achieve.

Think how that one word must have plagued the prophets. They lived in ancient days, but Satan was alive and well on planet Earth then as now. I can imagine . . .

Elijah.—Shortly after his greatest victory, Elijah leaves Mt. Carmel where the men of Baal have been defeated. He heads for Southern Judah, arrives there extremely tired after running a good part of the way, and he says to himself, "I can win any battle except the battle over Jezebel. If Queen Jezebel had never been born. God, I'm scared. She has her soldiers out to kill me. God, let me die."

Elisha.—The same man who has prayed for a double portion of the spirit of Elijah has received it, but is skeptical as God's power in his life is yet untested. Scared to death, just as he was about to perform his first miracle, he no doubt thought, "If only Elijah were alive."

Hosea.—God had just shared a tough assignment "Lord,"

he must have prayed, "Let me off the hook this time. You know the situation I have at home. I just can't do anything for you. I could and I would be the man you want me to be, if only I had a wife who was faithful to me."

Amos.—Called to be a prophet while serving in his vocation of gathering sycamore fruit, he pleads with God, "I would be glad to if only I had a better education."

Isaiah.—God asks, "Whom shall I send, and who will go for us?" The mind of Isaiah receives the temptation to reply, "You know you can always count on me, God, but the other day King Uzziah died. Now the whole nation may fall apart. We're all running a bit scared. But if our national affairs were in better shape . . ."

Ezekiel.—The brilliant young Jew, captured in Israel, held captive in Babylon has just been commanded by God to write a book. "I would not mind writing for you, Lord, if I was back in Jerusalem. Talk to me seventy years from now, and if we get out of this place, and I'm back home . . ."

Jeremiah.—He is being told by God he must preach the truth, even though the people will not appreciate the news of their coming judgment and captivity. For hours he wrestles with the thought, "I know what I better do. I'll strike a deal with God. I'll tell him that I'll do it provided he keeps me out of prison. But if I get into trouble and wind up in prison, I'm through listening to God.

Of course the prophets had thoughts like that! They were human, weren't they? Maybe not those same thoughts, but every way they turned they faced ifs. They became God's giants by refusing to believe those negative thoughts. When God speaks, calls, and assigns, a negative thought must not be tolerated.

Adoniram Judson, early missionary to Burma, faced seven unbelievably tough years. Number of converts—none. With a touch of sarcasm a "friend" asked, "What do you think the future holds for your work in Burma?" Judson replied, "The future is as bright as the promises of God!"

"If's" of an Apostle

Since Paul was possibly the greatest Christian since the time of Jesus, one might assume he had no "ifs" to overcome. Who said?

The *agnostic* "if" was probably Satan's first game with Paul. Atheism doubts with authority but agnosticism doubts by always coming up with more questions. Before the Damascus Road experience, the question marks of agnosticism kept his brain working overtime. "Relax, Paul, you've got a religion. You're a Hebrew of the Hebrews. If Jesus was for real, what could he do for someone with as much religion as you have?"

The *comparison* "if" may have been the second thought to get him. "I could never be like Stephen—he was something else. Why, he must have been the greatest Christian there ever was!"

God had no desire for Paul to be like Stephen, or Stephen like Paul! God wanted Paul to be Paul, but a totally yielded Paul.

The *appearance* "if" was no doubt his biggest hangup. There was nothing suave about Paul. His face may have been so common he could not stand himself. Second Corinthians 10:10 (Goodspeed) has Paul quoting back to the Corinthian people the exact crude words they had been saying about him. They had said, "His personal appearance is insignificant and as a speaker he amounts to nothing." The Amplified Translation has the Corinthians' comment, "His personality and bodily presence are weak, and his speech and delivery are utterly contemptible—of no account!"

Paul could not fake it. Night and day he was tempted to be nervous about his weaknesses. But he believed God could use even the uncommonly common face. It was a case of, "Here I am, God. If you can use me, great. It's up to you. I'm not much, in fact, I'm not anything, but maybe that way you will get all the credit for what's done through my life. Have a go at it, God!"

The ability "if" was the other half of the Corinthian slur. "As a speaker he amounts to nothing!" The sequence of events may have been—(1) the first night he heard their remark he wept; (2) the thought came that God could not use him because of his lack of ability; (3) he remembered that God had all power; (4) he realized it was not Paul but "Christ in Paul" which the world desperately needed to see; (5) he determined anew to let Christ use him in whatever way he could; and (6) what God thought about him was the important thing, not what somebody said.

It was A.D. 58 when he wrote 2 Corinthians and only two years later (A.D. 60) he was writing to the Colossians saying, "Christ worketh in me mightily" (Col. 1:29). Corinth's comments didn't stop Paul!

Thinking Straight

If . . . if . . . if—ad infinitum. Satan has one "if" to cause us to doubt God, another to cause us to doubt God's ability, another to destroy any thought that God could use weak vessels, and on and on it goes.

When a believer is Spirit-filled, however, new thoughts should engulf his brain:

(1) Jesus Christ lives in me.

(2) Jesus, with all the talent and ability he has—lives in me.

(3) Jesus, alive with power, indwells my life through the Holy Spirit.

(4) Jesus has always chosen to do great accomplishments through human vessels, provided they are fit for the Master's use—(2 Tim. 2:15-23).

(5) Jesus can accomplish through me provided I will be clean, forgiven, usable; filled with his fullness; ask him, allow him, and expect him to work through me.

One sentence turned Dwight L. Moody on. A speaker said, "The world has yet to see what God can do with one life totally yielded to Jesus Christ." Terrible in speech, poor in grammar, but with a heart hungry to be used, Moody said to himself, "By the grace of God I'll be that man."

Summary Questions

1. Why wait until all "if's" are removed? At least one "if" plagues every person. The greatest Christian you know—or the most handsome—or the most talented—or the greatest achiever—has some feature about himself he would love to see changed. But he relies on God's overcoming grace.
2. Why should the achiever always be someone else? God has a wonderful plan for your life.
3. Why should the one little word "if" be allowed to destroy the motivation the Holy Spirit has implanted within your life?

18
HOW TO GET MOTIVATED

Real motivation comes from a man knowing where
he's going and how he's going to get there. You
can see it in a man's eyes when he knows where
he's going.

—W. O. "Bill" Menefee
Home Care International

As he thinketh in his heart, so is he.
Proverbs 23:7

mo′ti-vate (mō′ti-vāt), v.t. To provide with a motive; to impel;
incite.

mo′tive (mō′tiv), n. [OF. motif, fr. ML. *motivus* moving, fr.
L. movere, motum, to move] 1. That within the individual,
rather than without, which incites him to motion; any idea,
need, emotion, or organic state that prompts to an action.

Webster is sharing several basic truths:

(1) Man frequently needs an outside force to move him
    (implied).
(2) The force which acts from without is not real motivation.
    It will last for awhile but something else must take over.
(3) Real motivation needs to come from within.
(4) Action is the end result of motivation, the goal sought
    for.

Necessity for Right Kind of Motivation

Spencer Goodreds tells of an old gentleman riding on the
ocean liner. When a storm blew up at sea a young woman,
leaning against the ship's rail, lost her balance and was thrown
overboard. Immediately another figure plunged into the waves
beside her and held her up until a life-boat rescued them.
To everyone's astonishment the hero was the oldest man on

the voyage—an octogenarian. That evening he was given a party in honor of his bravery. "Speech! Speech!" the other passengers cried.

The old gentleman rose slowly and looked around at the enthusiastic gathering. "There's just one thing I'd like to know," he said testily. "Who pushed me?"

It should not be too difficult for the intelligent man to understand why he needs to be acted upon. Both psychology and Scripture agree man needs a push and a pusher.

Psychology (the science of human and animal behavior) reminds us of the negative factors fixed within us, stored away somewhere within the twelve billion cells of the brain. Man has been taught "you can't," "you must not," and "someone else can do it better than you," until something of the basic push God implanted within has departed. This is not to say that all of the negatives we were taught while young have been necessarily bad. In fact, some of them have been startingly good. But now man needs a Bible—textbook direction as to what is good for him and what is not.

The average parent teaches in four ways—by his habits (which are not always good), by his words (not always wholesome), by his temperament (sometimes explosive), and by the whim of the moment!

"Friends" have done their share of feeding false information into the brain also. Boyce Evans is a traveling evangelist. I heard Boyce speak on the subject, "Why Worry?" The message stressed proper mental attitude and suggested, "Man is primarily the sum total of his thoughts." He shared an illustration from his seminary days.

Three ministerial students decided to use a friend as a guinea pig to test whether a man's physical makeup could be changed by his mental attitude. Their "victim" pastored a small country church each weekend and they set their trap when he returned to school at the start of the week.

"Didn't you sleep well last night?" the first friend asked, as the victim came whistling up the walk.

"Sure," he replied, and went on in.

A second man was stationed at the turn of the stairs. He started walking up the stairs with the pastor, and asked, "Bob, are you having trouble in your church?" Bob replied, "Well, I don't think so! At least not much."

The third man was stationed in the rear of the classroom. When Bob came in and took his seat, the third friend came over and said, "Friend, I am not a psychiatrist, but I can listen and if there is something you need to talk about, I would be glad to listen and try to help."

A bit of gloom settled over the victim's face. He answered, "Thank you, but I believe I can work it out." About forty-five minutes later he left class, whispering to one of the friends, "I'm going home. I'm sick."

Man is going to be motivated—the only question is *how*.

Kinds of Motivation

That which seeks to motivate from without is not real, lasting motivation.

Psychology tells us that man has basic organic drives—drives which must be satisfied. Drives such as hunger and thirst, activity, rest, sex, physical labor, the body craving for a certain temperature range, all fall into this physiological category.

Self-satisfaction of these drives is important and if God instilled these drives, he apparently intended they would find their outlet. But in every case he either built in saturation points or else gave specific governing rules. It is interesting that if there was not a Bible (book with specific direction as to how to act and what to do) man would have to invent one. So God gave us one—with wisdom straight from the storehouse of his knowledge—and all for our good.

Aside from the physiological needs, man also has psychological needs. He longs for accomplishment of tasks and achievement of goals. Fundamental to his makeup is a desire to achieve. Even the infant in the crib expresses satisfaction when he has achieved.

At this point we need to be reminded that behavior is caused. "A stimulus leads to some sort of inter-action with an organism which is followed by behavior that we call a response. This response is also fed back to the organism as a stimulus." [1]

The S-O-R (stimulus-organism-response) idea continually sends us searching for the right stimulus to motivate man. Consider a business corporation seeking to motivate an employee. What approach would be used?

To motivate man, a corporation invariably uses fear.—Industry must lay down the rules of a job and rules invariably imply fear! A job description is placed in a man's hand. He is told, "This is the job to be done." The implication is that if the job assignment is not met, the person is fired. This type of reality therapy has him "living under the hammer." He works, he gives the desired response, but as time goes on something additional is needed.

Industry may also stimulate the man through hope of reward.—Reward (long term benefits, salary raise, or both) is great—for awhile. Let a blue Monday come, when the employee is coming apart at the seams, and the hope of reward, whether given at age sixty-five or in tomorrow's paycheck, seems to make no difference. He slows down in his work and unless something additional happens, may well walk off the job—unmotivated.

Real motivation is motivation of the spirit.—When a man is motivated (moved toward action) from within, he will far surpass any achievements he would otherwise have accomplished. Which brings us back exactly to what Mr. Webster was saying in his definitions. Prompting toward an action needs to work from the inside out.

Paul J. Meyer, President of Success Motivation Institute, states; "No matter who you are or what your age may be, if you want to achieve permanent, sustaining success, the motivation that will drive you toward that goal must come from within. It must be personal, deep-rooted and a part of your inner-most thoughts. All other motivation, the excitement of a crowd, the stimulation of a pep-talk, the exhilaration of a passing circumstance is external and temporary. It will not last."

Henry Ward Beecher suggested, "God made man to go by motives and he will not go without them, anymore than a boat without steam, or a balloon without gas." Mack Douglas adds, "Find what motivates men and we can touch the button, we can turn the key that makes men achieve miracles."

Back to the example of the factory worker. When the employer shared the job description and suggested they would be thrilled to have him as an employee, but only so long as he carried out the requirements, he was using motivation by fear. "Was it wrong for him to do it?" Not at all. Some would call it fear motivation, but an even better definition would be fact motivation. He would do the job, or he would be fired, and sharing the truth is a help, not a hindrance. The employee should forever be grateful the facts were shared (and the implications of dismissal) at the time of hiring—rather than not know about his job expectations and discover them later after he was fired.

Fear motivation in relation to accomplishment is not wrong, provided it is based on fact.

Is there anything wrong with reward motivation? Of course not. Again the same requirement must be met—the hope of reward must be based on fact. Reward motivation (offer of raise in salary or advancement in position) is absolutely wrong, even if it gets more work out of the man, if the employer cannot produce the reward.

Motivation of the spirit (attitude motivation) is, however, the best kind of motivation and cannot be surpassed by any other. S-O-R (stimulation-organism-response) has been set in motion but this time the response is a response from love. There is a "want-to" changed on the inside. A man is motivated to work harder, achieve more, because his heart is in the company! And what employer isn't searching for that in his workers!

"How do you change a man on the inside?" becomes the
$64,000 question. What kind of power can remake man? What
is there that causes him to love the assembly line in spite
of the fact it is boring and repetitious? Only a motivation of
the spirit. When that has happened, a man is impelled to
respond whether or not circumstances are favorable.

Motivation by Application of the Bible

The secret to real motivation has been in the Bible for
centuries. Not only does the Bible teach that man must be
spurred to action from the inside, but God even sends his Holy
Spirit to dwell within and provide the motivation.

The same is true whether we speak of the physiological
needs or the psychological.

God's help in the physiological area is twofold: first, he
lays down laws which make for man's ultimate happiness;
second, he thrusts his power within, enabling man to be able
to keep those laws.

In the psychological area, the story of motivation is the
same. As the power of God resides in the life through the
Holy Spirit, man is motivated to accomplishment. The one
who daily reads God's Word, and daily applies the "Three
C's" (see chap. 15) discovers fantastic inner motivation.

In summary, the Bible attempts to direct man in some
stunning principles of achievement. Too often we have considered that the Bible knew nothing about success and accomplishment of goals. When, in fact, if we heed its commands,
we will discover every command was for a purpose.

Principles of Achievement

1. Man is meant to achieve. Immediately after creation,
man was told to be fruitful, multiply, replenish the earth, and
subdue it.

2. Man must be motivated to achieve. Satan has many ways
of implanting negatives in the mind, and the path of least
resistance is the most well-trodden path.

3. Inner change is the beginning of the motivation process. Jesus designed the inner change idea as "being converted and becoming as little children" and as "being born again." Paul said to the Corinthians, "If any man be in Christ, he is a new creature. Old things are passed away, behold all things are become new." Salvation is when we are "created in Christ Jesus unto good works" (Eph. 2:10).

4. Motivation must be through daily repetition, feeding the brain with habits, thought patterns, and desires. "Pray without ceasing" and "rejoice in the Lord always" are not idle commands. The psalmist and Daniel each had daily habits of prayer, men in Berea searched the Scriptures daily (Acts 17:11), and the disciples went about sharing Christ with others on a daily basis (Acts 5:42). Repetition is essential in motivation.

5. Goal-setting is the necessary pointer to keep man moving in the right direction. From the time Jesus began his public ministry he seemed to have his goals set—he would please God, defeat the devil, and die for the sins of man. Six months prior to Calvary, he stated that he "must go into Jerusalem, and suffer, . . . and be killed, and be raised the third day" (Matt. 16:21). Earlier he had stated that the goal of his ministry was "to seek and to save that which was lost" (Luke 19:10).

6. Believe in God's power to accomplish through you is a must. Napoleon Hill said, "Whatever the mind of man can believe, it can achieve." Jesus said, "with God all things are possible" (Matt. 19:26) and again, "If thou canst believe, all things are possible to him that believeth" (Mark 9:23).

---

[1] F. Marshall Brown, F. K. Berrien, David L. Russell, *Applied Psychology* (New York: The Macmillan Co., 1966), p. 380.

19
MOTIVATION—EVEN IN TIMES OF SUFFERING

I am filled with comfort, I am exceeding joyful in all our tribulation.
—The Apostle Paul
2 Corinthians 7:4

There wouldn't be a brook without rocks.
—S. M. Lockridge

A cartoon showed a man and a woman at a counter marked "Educational Toys." A clerk was showing them a box filled with odd-shaped fragments. "It's designed to prepare children for today's complex world. No matter how they put it together, it doesn't come out right."

Right at this point someone might plead, "Is this book going to be like some others I've read? Don't just talk about the good. What about my suffering? Nothing in life's puzzle makes sense to me due to my difficulties. Where does that fit in?"

"You see, I can believe God is interested in my success when my definition fits his. I can believe he is interested in helping me achieve goals he helps me set. But why my pain? I'm his!"

"If God wants me to live on the mountaintop, to possess an inner thrill and radiance, to be surrounded by joy and peace, then I should have no suffering. Right?"

Wrong.

Suffering definitely relates to success and motivation. But not in the way the average man thinks.

Life Without Pain?

If you could have one wish, what would it be? High on the list of answers received to such a question would be, "Just give me life without pain." You wouldn't want that!

113

Little Beverly Smith, born in Akron, Ohio, almost never cried. She never cried when she fell down; she never cried when she bumped her head; she didn't even cry when she burned her hand on a hot stove. She cried only when she was hungry or angry.

The doctors soon discovered that she had a defect in the central nervous system for which no cure is known. She could not feel pain. The doctors told the mother she must watch Beverly constantly; the baby might break a bone and continue using it until it could not be set properly; she might develop appendicitis without nature's usual warning of pain. Spanking her to make her more careful about hot stoves and knives would do her no good; she wouldn't feel it. Life without pain would be perpetually dangerous.[1]

And up until now, you've no reason to expect you'll ever have life without pain. Only the abnormal never hurt.

Jesus said, "In the world ye shall have tribulation." That's not the same as saying that you might have it. You positively shall. Tribulation, trouble, pain, and perplexity is a very normal part of life.

Of all people, Christians are certainly not exempt. If any person came to Christ believing life would automatically be a bed of roses, he received quite a surprise! Years ago, one of the professors at the Seminary used to tell his young ministerial students, "Boys, be kind to everybody. Everybody's got problems."

A study of the life of the apostle Paul would indicate that he had more than most anyone! Second Corinthians 11:23-27 reveals that on different occasions he was stoned, beaten with rods, shipwrecked, and one time left for dead! Instead of life being easy, life was tough. He further said he had been "in perils of waters, in perils of robbers, in perils by mine own countrymen, in perils by the heathen, in perils in the city, in perils in the wilderness, in perils in the sea, in perils among false brethren; in weariness and painfulness, in watchings often, in hunger and thirst, in fastings often, in cold and nakedness." If God meant to exempt Christians from problems, he forgot to tell Paul about it!

A life without pain is apparently not God's intention.

Joy in Spite of Circumstances

Furthermore, the Christian is commanded to be joyful. Instead of joy ceasing when trouble begins, joy is commanded in the midst of and in spite of suffering.

Jesus seemed to begin the idea of New Testament times. As a part of his Sermon on the Mount, he proposed, "Blessed are ye, when men shall revile you, and persecute you, and shall say all manner of evil against you falsely, for my sake. Rejoice and be exceeding glad" (Matt. 5:11-12). In the last week before the cross, Jesus said, "In the world ye shall have tribulation: but be of good cheer" (John 16:33).

From a Philippian jail cell, God inspired Paul to write, sharing not despondency, but thrill. "Finally, my brethren, rejoice in the Lord" (Phil. 3:1). "Rejoice in the Lord away: and again I say, Rejoice" (4:4).

In other writings, the same theme is echoed. The situation or circumstance surrounding the writing seemed to make no difference—the command was still the same. "Rejoice evermore" (1 Thess. 5:16). "In every thing give thanks: for this is the will of God in Christ Jesus concerning you" (v. 18). "The fruit of the Spirit is love, joy, peace, longsuffering" (Gal. 5:22).

John may seem even more shocking on the idea of suffering than Paul, particularly when the background is studied. Scholars tell us he did his writing about A.D. 95 when the persecutions of Emperor Domitian were in full swing. History reveals that by then approximately fifty percent of the population of the Roman empire were slaves. Slaves in the Roman world were not considered people (*personae*) but things (*res*). And to an audience in which at least 50 percent were slaves, God says, "These things are written that your joy may be full!" (1 John 1:4).

The conclusion can only be one—God expects the believer to have joy no matter what!

The Anguish of Defeat

One type of suffering often overlooked in a discussion of the problem is the suffering caused by defeat. Failure has to be spelled with capital letters in all our vocabularies. Who hasn't suffered because of himself?

Paul did. Prior to his conversion he failed God in a number of ways. To say that he later hated himself for previous actions would be the understatement of the year. But believing in the thoroughness of God's forgiveness gave Paul a brand new beginning.

In the matter of a saved person disappointing God, John Mark has to be one of two classic examples. Acts 13:13 tells the sad account of his starting on the first missionary journey, and then turning back. More than that, his action almost split a beautiful friendship between Barnabas and Paul. But bounce, did he bounce! When Paul writes his last letter prior to death, he urges Timothy to bring Mark "for he is profitable to me for the ministry" (2 Tim. 4:11). In addition, God used him to write a book of the Bible!

Simon Peter denied Jesus, but Jesus forgave him. For Simon not to forgive himself would have compounded his sin. He learned to believe Jesus, accept his forgiveness, and the once-defeated Simon became the preacher of Pentecost, and God's leader in the thrilling events to follow.

When Satan has won one victory, some throw up the white flag of surrender and let him have the whole war! Not Simon Peter!

If Mark and Peter, and even Paul could forget "the things that are behind," so can you. Just don't forget them until you have confessed your sin to God and received his promised forgiveness and cleansing according to 1 John 1:9.

Tears and Brokenness

What about tears? If a man is a success, does this mean

he will never weep again?

Contrariwise, the successful man will be a concerned man. He will be concerned about the will of God, the walk of his friends, and the way the world is going. the more successful he is, the more concerned he will be! A person can weep and be joyful at the same time. Joy is a fixed state of the heart, whereas tears are a God-given emotional outlet. One may be joyful over a thousand blessings God has given, plus joyful and excited about being a Christian, but when he stands in the presence of God he may well become broken.

Pity the poor man who thinks he is so successful he cannot show concern. He is not successful—he is proud, haughty, calloused, self-righteous, and blind to human need.

God's great men have always been men of concern. They have known joy as a state of the heart but have, at the same time, been brokenhearted over conditions around them.

David wept over his son Absalom, Jeremiah wept over a nation, Jesus wept over Jerusalem, and Paul shed many tears in Ephesus over a space of three years. God's promise to the concerned soul-winner is, "He that goeth forth and weepeth, bearing precious seed, shall doubtless come again with rejoicing, bringing his sheaves with him" (Ps. 126:6).

Fullness of joy will never be discovered by one who runs from human need. God will resist the proud, but give grace to the humble! (Jas. 4:6; 1 Pet. 5:5).

The Big Jobs

God is on the lookout for people he can trust with giant problems. Giant tasks are everywhere in this world. There is, however, a prerequisite before you can be chosen for this job.

Allow an explanation.

Recently the Lockheed L-1011 TriStar airplane was finished and the company began 18 months of rigorous testing costing $1.5 billion dollars. To test the strength of the jetliner, Lockheed has an airplane torture rack. It bends, twists, and pulls the structure of the plane to simulate the roughest treatment it will encounter in commercial operation.

Hydraulic jacks, electronic sensors, and a computer put the airplane through a fatigue test for a minimum of 36,000 flights. A lower wind joint of the jet liner underwent five lifetimes of simulated flight without failure, amounting to more than a hundred years of airline service.

Thirty-one 250-gallon water tanks were placed inside one of the test aircraft. The water tanks are connected by a series of pipes and pumps for transferring the aircraft's center of gravity in flight. Flight tests showed that the aircraft could handle a wider range of gravity than predicted by designers.

One of the planes was flown into ice clouds by test pilots. They wanted to check operation of the anti-ice systems and see how the aircraft would respond to ice accretion. The flight test crew permitted heavy chunks of ice to break away from the nose of the aircraft and enter the rear mounted engine. They permitted heavy ice build-ups on one wing while keeping the other ice-free.[2]

That plane has been through it! I wouldn't mind flying on it, would you? Life is sometimes like that, and the testing times no less easy.

But wouldn't it be just like God . . . to take one look at the totally yielded Christian who had walked through sufferings and tensions, take another look at a giant task which desperately needed doing, then cast his eye back toward the Christian and write across his life—tested; trustworthy; yielded; motivated from within; ready for the big job!

---
[1] Donald Grey Barnhouse, *Let Me Illustrate* (Westwood, New Jersey: Fleming H. Revell Co., 1967), p. 21.
[2] *Airline Passenger Association News* (Summer/Fall 1972), pp. 26-30.

PART SIX:
EXCITEMENT PLUS—THE RESULT
OF PROPER MOTIVATION

20
EXCITEMENT PLUS IN CHRISTIANITY

Marcus Aurelius said, "A man's life is what his thoughts make it." The Bible says, "As a man thinketh in his heart, so is he." Can you even dare to dream what might happen if you were to begin getting excited in your thinking?

God has put Christ in us, the Bible says. Then it takes little or no imagination to believe that God has put in us the ability to do anything he wants done through us.

Motivation leads to excitement. Find the person who has a daily motivation of the Spirit and you will find an excited person.

"I shall not forget," Dr. Bill Bright has said, "as a young Christian, I read from a famous New Testament scholar, Dr. James Stewart of Edinburgh. I memorized what he said, it moved me so much. He said, 'If we could but show the world that being committed to Christ is no tame humdrum, sheltered monotony, but the most thrilling, exciting adventure the human spirit could ever know!' " Daily inner motivation by God's Spirit results in excitement plus!

Southwestern Baptist Seminary's warm-hearted president, Dr. Robert Naylor, addressed 7,000 young people on a July night at Falls Creek Encampment near Davis, Oklahoma. His theme each night of the week had been "What Do You Think of Jesus?" When he came to the last night, he began his message with the words, "I've been asking you all week what you think of Jesus. I want to tell you what I think of him. I just can't wait to walk the next mile with him." Excitement plus!

Spiritually hungry, a nightclub entertainer drifted into a revival meeting in Alabama recently. When the service had concluded, she shared with the pastor, "This is the most unique and exciting thing I have ever seen in my life."

Christianity has always been that way. It was born in the heart of God with the intention of being exciting, thrilling, and an answer to the needs of man.

Our generation shall give account to God if we have lacked enthusiasm. Someone sadly commented that modern preachers have been able to do what no one has been able to do for nearly 2,000 years—make Christ appear dull. If that is true of any preacher, it is unbelievably tragic. The watermark our generation must leave behind was rightly stated by Dr. Stewart—Christianity is the most thrilling, exciting adventure the human spirit could ever know.

Sources of Excitement

Being convinced that God wants us to be happy, motivated, excited about life, the question arises, "How?" Already we have noted that true motivation has come from within. Excitement is similar. It cannot be faked. False excitement ruins character. Honest excitement builds character. There are six basic sources of excitement:

1. The excitement of being needed
2. The excitement of being usable
3. The excitement of being on the winning team
4. The excitement of the "greater-than" concept
5. The excitement of expectation (faith)
6. The excitement of goal-setting and goal-reaching

Now for our study of excitement. These sources could well be memorized. They bear oft-repeating.

1. Excitement comes from being needed.

Consider the person who has been defeated. He imagines he is not needed. He believes the devil's lie. Wise was the man who said, "It makes no difference who you are or what you are, or how discouraged you may be, if you are still alive, God has a purpose for your life."

James McConkey, whose 1918 writing of *The Three-Fold*

Secret of the Holy Spirit remains a classic, has another work entitled, *The Surrendered Life*, written in 1903. He says:

The Lord hath need of thee, saved one. Trade, with all its rush, and fever, and wear, and waste, lays its hands upon the Christian and says curtly: "I need you to plan, think, toil, accumulate, and die in my service." Society, too, asserts its claim, and says: "I need you with your wit, beauty, talents and accomplishments to shine in the brilliant circles of fashion, and will give you pleasure without limit if you will yield to me." Professional life lays its hand on him and says: "I need you to adorn your chosen calling, and will gratify your highest ambitions if you will come." But there comes a voice, softly floating down twenty vanished centuries, a voice which whispers to every redeemed child of God in the hour when wealth, and pleasure, and ambition have failed to satisfy his secret longings; a voice which is true today as of old: "The Lord hath need of thee."

There are so many people in the world to be helped, and each of us can be used to help others. In China alone there are so many people that if those hundreds of millions were to be lined up four abreast and begin marching in columns around the world, the line would never come to an end. In Jesus' day there were 250 million people in the world; in A.D. 1600, 500 million; in A.D. 1900, one and one-half billion; and by A.D. 2000 there will be 6 billion.

When a philosopher found himself in a concentration camp, and spent several years watching his friends struggle to stay alive, he concluded, "He who has a why to live can live with almost any how."

Your why is that Christ needs you. Christ needs you in a world where people are falling apart. God, in his mighty plan, thrust you into the most exciting and troubled generation ever. There are people you can reach no one else can ever reach. The Lord hath need of thee!

2. Excitement comes from being usable.

The thrilling life is the usable life. The first-century disciples also gained a great deal of excitement because they knew they were usable. They stayed on their knees until they were. Then they expected God to use them.

In our honest moments we know God cannot use an unclean vessel. When sin is confessed, and the vessel is clean, the individual feels usable. Paul exhorts Timothy to "purge himself" that he might be "a vessel unto honour, sanctified, meet for the master's use, and prepared unto every good work" (2 Tim. 2:21). Just as sin in the life removes every trace of excitement, confession and cleansing can restore it.

Someone recently game me an outline entitled "The Man God Uses." The list is excellent for periodic checkup.

THE MAN GOD USES
1. He has but one great purpose in life.
2. He has, by God's grace, removed every hindrance from his life.
3. He has placed himself absolutely at God's disposal.
4. He has learned how to prevail in prayer.
5. He is a student of the Word.
6. He has a vital, living message for the lost world.
7. He is a man of faith who expects results.
8. He works in the anointing of the Holy Spirit.

Some years ago, two missionaries in China were talking. One was praying, "Lord, use me." The other said, "Stop praying like that. It's not any of your business whether the Lord uses you or not. You just get usable."

Vance Havner remarks, "Stop praying, 'Lord, use me' and get usable and the Lord will wear you out!"

3. Excitement comes from the "winning team concept."

Attend a football game and watch the crowd. At the outset everybody is excited. But soon excitement grows or lags depending on whose team is winning.

The resurrection of Christ turned eleven disheartened disciples around. They had previously thought they were on the winning team, but when even the grave could not hold Christ, they knew they were on the winning team! And their excitement grew by the moment. "With boldness" (Acts 4:31), "with great power" (4:33), "full of faith and power" (6:8), and "filled with joy" (13:52) became common descriptive terms in the book of Acts. Some even said they were turning the world upside down—actually they were turning it right-side up! They were excited and had reason to be—they were on the winning team.

Consider the book of Revelation. Written in one of the dark hours of persecution, the theme is "Get excited—we're on the winning team!"

4. Excitement comes from the "greater-than" concept.

Another thought that leaps from the lives of the first-century disciples is the "greater-than" concept. How could a few men (fishermen, tax collectors, common laborers, and the like) be charged with enough enthusiasm to take on the first-century Roman world? They believed (1) Christ lived in them and (2) Christ was greater-than! They went about thinking, "Greater is he that is in you, than he that is in the world" (1 John 4:4). Christ had given them an advanced preview of that thought in his last conversation with them (John 14:17-23).

The promises of God are not all past or future tense. Check them out for the here-and-now.

"The Lord is the strength of my life" (Ps. 27:1).

"Thanks be to God, which giveth us the victory through our Lord Jesus Christ" (1 Cor. 15:57).

"We are more than conquerors through him that loved us" (Rom. 8:37).

"My grace is sufficient for thee" (2 Cor. 12:9).

"[Our God] is able to do exceeding abundantly above all that we ask or think" (Eph. 3:20).

"The Lord is my shepherd" (Ps. 23:1).

"There is therefore now no condemnation to them which are in Christ Jesus" (Rom. 8:1).

"God is able to make all grace abound toward you" (2 Cor. 9:8).

"Greater is he that is in you, than he that is in the world" (1 John 4:4).

5. Excitement comes from expectation (faith).

Jim Hylton excitingly comments, "You can't write checks

on the Bank of Heaven until you know your account. But once you know what kind of account you have in heaven, you can go and start writing checks on it (on your privileges). But if you don't know what kind of account you have you are not going to be drawing on the resources of God."

Imagine waking up each morning, thinking, "I can draw on the resources of God!" Of course you can—if your account is right and up-to-date.

The person God will choose to use will be the one who has faith and expects results. God is insulted by those who hold a "little God" concept, yet the biggest thing millions ask him to do each day is "bless the food."

Henry Ford said, "Whether or not you think you can, you're right!" I would add, "Whether or not you think God can do it through you, you're right!" If you refuse to honor God enough to believe him for big things, he will go on only blessing your food.

If a man refuses to believe God for big things, let him at least not blame God when nothing happens. Let him wonder no longer why excitement never comes his way—excitement comes from expectation.

6. Excitement comes from goal-setting and goal-reaching.

Not failure, but low aim, is our crime. Perhaps the subject of goals demands a study all by itself.

We'll tackle that in the next chapter.

Christ in You

You've just learned six good sources of excitement. Don't forget them.

Could we summarize all six statements by saying—You have every right to be excited if Christ is in your life. Christ in you, the hope of glory! (Col. 1:27). He is the—

Source of your being needed,
　Reason you can be usable.
　　Coach of the winning team,
　　　Secret to the "greater-than" concept,

Author of your expectation, plus being the
Power in goal setting and goal reaching.
Stay close to him and you'll get excited. Follow him from afar and you'll drift into a dull, routine-like existence. You don't want to exist, you want to live. You don't want to just think excitement, you want to live excitement.

Every saved person can rejoice—"Christ in me? I just can't wait to walk the next mile with him!"

21
GOAL-SETTING AND GOD

> There came a time in my life when I earnestly
> prayed: "God, I want your power!"
> Time wore on and the power did not come.
> One day the burden was more than I could bear.
> "God, why haven't you answered that prayer?"
> God seemed to whisper back his simple reply.
> "With plans no bigger than yours, you don't need
> my power."
> —Carl Bates

> This one thing I do, forgetting those things which
> are behind, and reaching forth unto those things
> which are before, I press toward the mark for the
> prize of the high calling of God in Christ Jesus.
> —Goal of the apostle Paul

Some years ago a headline told of 300 whales which suddenly died. The whales were pursuing sardines and found themselves marooned in a bay. Frederick Brown Harris commented, "The small fish lured the sea giants to their death. . . . They came to their violent demise by chasing small ends, by prostituting vast powers for insignificant goals."

What kinds of goals do you have? Answer that question honestly for me, and I can tell you how much excitement you have in your life.

Christians, of all people, need to wrestle with the concept of goals. When a salesman sat in my office to talk with me about success, he asked me to take a sheet of paper, and a pencil, and write down three goals. I did, but I would have been embarrassed had he appeared on the scene some years back. Like many Christians I know, I had no goals. And I reached all I had!

Problems of Goal-setting

"But I have problems with this thing of goal-setting!" several voices quickly say. Relax. Probably everyone either has a problem or once had a problem. But what's yours?

Problem No. 1 in Goal-setting: The problem of finding the correct concept of Christian contentment.

"You want to know my problem in setting goals?" *Dedicated Darla* inquires. "I read the Bible quite a bit and consider myself fairly knowledgeable. I can give you three reasons as to why I've hesitated to set goals. My reasons are all Scripture verses."

"Be content with such things as ye have" (Heb. 13:5).

"I have learned, in whatsoever state I am, therewith to be content" (Phil. 4:11).

"But godliness with contentment is great gain" (1 Tim. 6:6).

Rather difficult to argue with the Scriptures, isn't it? "So that means I should set no goals. Right?" Darla inquires. Hm-m-m. . . .

Let's study Darla's situation. She is absolutely right in her desire to obey God's Word. The Bible was written to provide wonderful instruction and one good rule Darla has learned is to always obey God's Word. She has also learned that every rule God has given is, in reality, for her own good. Her mistake is in interpretation. Contentment does not mean what Darla has interpreted it to mean. Hence her error of setting no goals.

Those who wrestle with the meaning of contentment could come up with two possibilities. So how about a multiple choice test. Which of the two would you circle as being correct?

The meaning of contentment is: (circle the correct one)

1. I should have my desires limited to that which I already have, and that which I have already achieved.

2. I should have my desires limited to that which I am convinced God wants me to have, and that which God wants me to achieve.

There's a world of difference in those two ideas of contentment! The first spells laziness, the second spells lordship! Christian contentment majors on the lordship of Christ.

Lordship (having Christ in the control tower) should be the primary prerogative in the study of every Christian concept.

The Christian should decide that whatever he does in the area of setting goals or not setting goals, he will do under the lordship of Christ. You can stake your life on the fact that however God meant for us to interpret those verses, the outcome would not belittle the lordship of Christ. Everything a Christian does must center around having Christ in the control tower.

If Christ is in the control tower, what will my Christian contentment mean? Contentment must not be interpreted as laziness, indifference, unconcern, apathy, prayerlessness, or failure to witness, because godliness and contentment are to be a part of the same life. However, there is a concept which will not belittle the meaning of contentment, or do away with godliness, or take Christ's prerogatives as Lord of the life. Allow me to submit what I believe was Paul's concept of Christian contentment.

1. I am thrilled today with what God has given me. I am wonderfully satisfied.

2. My thrill today is by no means a guarantee that God intends I be thrilled tomorrow with the same things.

3. I want my desires limited (if need be) to that which God wants me to have, and that which God wants me to achieve.

4. I also want my desires stretched (if need be) to that which I am convinced God wants me to have, and that which God wants me to achieve.

There's a picture of contentment under the lordship of Christ. Whether the desires will need to be limited or stretched will be a matter of daily wisdom achieved in time alone with God.

God may more often require a stretching rather than a shrinking! In fact, he rebukes us for our failure to stretch, for not thinking big. "Ye have not, because ye ask not!" (Jas.

4:2).

Goal-setting for the Christian is simply planned, organized, stretching under the lordship of Christ.

Problem No. 2 in Goal-Setting: The problem of previous defeat.

Defeated Dan has a different kind of problem. He doesn't mind setting goals—he has just never reached any.

As a result, the defeat and despair he feels within results in a downcast spirit in everything he does. It even shows on his face.

Defeated Dan does have a problem—a very real problem. Dr. Clyde M. Narramore spent years as a consultant in research and guidance for the schools of Los Angeles County. Currently, Dr. Narramore is founder and president of the Rosemead (California) Graduate School of Psychology, a school which trains graduate Christian psychologists. He shares his pertinent words:

> It's not easy to be enthusiastic about the future when one has not been successful in the past. Failure dims our outlook. Tomorrows seldom look bright if our yesterdays have been marred by dissatisfaction. . . . There's nothing like failure to kill incentive and ambition. People don't mind working hard when the reward is accomplishment. But to work without results is no better than aimlessly marking time—going 'round and 'round in the same old rut, getting nowhere. Like a donkey on a treadmill. And that's when life becomes the "same old grind." Yes, it takes more than striving to develop a well adjusted personality. It also takes some arriving.[1]

Should the defeated person be advised to never again set goals? Or is the problem not with goal-setting but with improper goal-setting?

Goals Dan chose were too big, unattainable. Not reaching any of the goals, he soon felt he couldn't do what others do. "I'm just a natural-born failure," he said to himself.

Parents who are perfectionists may have led to such a condition. Parental goals may always have been so big, so unattainable, that Dan felt he was never able to "just enjoy being me, for Jesus' sake."

Or Dan may have been overly ambitious. Not praying about his goals, maybe he chose some out of pure selfishness. "I'll show them who I am and what I can do." God just could not bless that. Result—a defeated person.

The defeated and downcast person should first go to his knees in prayer. Let him lay down all his previous goals, surrendering them to the lordship of Christ. He should confess his sin of trying to "heap riches unto himself" (if that was his sin), or the sin of forgetting to use the head God gave and blundering by setting what should have been a yearly goal as his monthly goal.

Let him set a goal for something he knows he can attain this week—he will have to stretch a bit—yes, but a goal he knows he can attain. At week's end, to use Dr. Narramore's words, he will not be *striving* but *arriving*. Next week his goal can be a bit bigger, but let him not bite off impossible chunks and develop give-up-itis.

Problem No. 3 in Goal-Setting: The problem of fuzziness in the financial area.

Read a dozen books on goal-setting and you'll understand the problem *Moneymad Merle* developed. Half of the books convinced him that anyone who would buy the book and apply the rules should soon be a millionaire. Merle didn't make it! He even began to blame God for lousing him up! After all, some guys were making it.

The question comes as to whether God is interested in Merle's finances. Let's switch from Merle to you. You may wonder if God is interested in your finances. Certainly.

How do you know? God is interested in you! You have to spend a lot of time thinking about finances. If you believed in worry, you would spend a lot of time worrying about them. In other words, they are your concern. God urges you to cast "all your care [concern] upon him; for he careth for you" (1 Pet. 5:7). To care about your concerns, God would have to care about your finances.

God is probably not at all interested in making you a millionaire. Nine of ten millionaires have no time for God—just time for money. In other words, money ruins their sense of values. it's a rare man who is not ruined by a lot of money. God is not interested in ruining a man's values, or home relationships, or giving him a bighead, or in making him spend all his time figuring out how to make more. God has helped a few men become millionaires, knowing their millions could be used for his glory. But interested in ruining a man? Not God.

Of course, neither does God want his children to be always looking as if God cannot properly provide for them. Believers should be good advertisements for God, not bad ones. The God who owns the cattle on a thousand hills will care for his own. He always provides, but whether we spend what we have correctly is another matter.

There is a vast difference between needs and wants. The promise of God is that he will supply your needs (Phil. 4:19). Many a person has gotten in serious financial trouble because God supplied enough for his needs, but the individual used it to satisfy his wants.

Need financial advice? God's success book suggests that we (1) Put God first in our lives, not "things" (Matt. 6:33); (2) Believe God for his help in meeting our needs (Phil. 4:19); (3) Pray about even the smallest matter of concern (Phil. 4:6; 1 Pet. 5:7); (4) Pay debts promptly (Prov. 3:28); (5) Give God at least one tenth of our income (Mal. 3:8-10); (6) Avoid surety, or the guaranteeing of another's note (Prov. 11:15; 17:18; 22:26); (7) Refuse to love money (1 Tim. 6:10;) (8) Work for our income (Ex. 20:9; 2 Thess. 3:10).

Should a person think of setting goals in the financial area? That depends—will God or the individual get the glory from attainment? Will the lives of others be wonderfully blessed if you are blessed? Will people be reached for Christ because of your blessing? It is not wrong to have material goals—just make sure God is the one who gives them to you rather than you giving them to God. Basically, we are all tempted to be selfish.

Pray about your financial situation. Ask God about your goals. After all, he's the captain in charge and he would not want you to have anything which could later hurt you.

Problem No. 4 in Goal-Setting: The problem of paralyzing mediocrity.

Now for the biggest problem of all. More problems develop in the goal-setting area over this one hangup than over all the rest. Whereas Defeated Dan had killed himself with setting goals too big, Easygoing Ernest sets goals so small they are dishonoring and displeasing to the God who made him. God not only has a problem with Easygoing Ernest, his kind may pose the biggest problem God has.

PATIENT: tell me Doc, in plain English, just what's wrong
           with me.

DOC: You're just plain lazy.

PATIENT: Now could you give me the medical term to tell
           my friends?

There is no excuse for laziness, apathy, or indifference in a believer's life. A majority of those who have no goals may be guilty of paralyzing mediocrity.

Goals and God's Giants

People who have power with God are not afraid of goals. They thrive on them. God apparently has no fear of them—he assigns them.

Abraham's goal was to follow God anywhere, to the end of the earth if necessary, and gather people around him who would walk by faith. Moses' goal was to rescue all the Jews from bondage and lead them toward the Promised Land. David's goal was to save his people from the Philistines, even if he had to fight Goliath himself. Elijah's goal was to destroy Baal worship in Israel. No risk was too great, no odds too big. Elisha's goal was to have a double portion of the spirit and power of Elijah resting upon him, and he would not be denied. Christ's goal—he stated it in two ways—"For the Son of man is come to seek and to save that which is lost" (Luke 19:10), and "I am come that they might have life, and that they might have it more abundantly" (John 10:10).

A man without goals comes to the end of life only to discover that the bulk of his life history can be summarized by

> 20 years sleeping
> 5 years dressing and shaving
> 3 years waiting on others
> 1 year on the telephone
> 4 months tying his shoes, and
> 6 years watching television.

Without goals the routines of life becomes the ruts of life!

Even books of the Bible have goals. When God inspired John to write several books of the Bible, the goal was established. These are written, that ye might believe that Jesus is the Christ, the Son of God; and that believing ye might have life through his name" (John 20:31). When 1 John was penned, a twofold goal was shared: "These things write we unto you, that your joy may be full" (1:4); and "These things have I written unto you . . . that ye may know that ye have eternal life" (5:13).

Second John (v. 12) again shares God's goal to the recipients: "Having many things to write unto you, I would not write with paper and ink: but I trust to come unto you, and speak face to face, that our joy may be full!" The goal of 3 John is "Beloved, I wish above all things that thou mayest prosper and be in health, even as thy soul prospereth" (v. 2).

The importance of goals is underlined by Dr. Howard G. Hendricks. "I have never met a Christian who sat down and planned to live a mediocre life. But if you keep going in the direction in which you are moving, you may land there." [2]

Test Your Goals

It is not enough to have goals, the Christian should also test them. Here is a "Christian's Check List for Testing Goals."

1. Do all my goals fit into the context of my written, stated purpose for my life (life-long goal).
2. Have I been honest enough to set goals in every area of life, believing God is interested in the total "me"—spiritual area? recreational area? professional area? social area? educational and intellectual area? family relationship area? financial area?
3. Have I developed long-range, short-range, and immediate goals? Have I developed them in that order so the long-range goal will pre-determine my other goals?
4. Can my goals glorify God or are they selfish in nature?
5. Did I ask God for his wisdom and guidance before I attempted to establish these goals?
6. Would Jesus Christ be willing to be Lord of my life and preside over the reaching of goals such as mine?
7. If I am thoroughly convinced these are God-given goals, then cannot I expect his power to work in the achievement of these goals?

A few years ago T. B. Maston shared some excellent questions and tests. Although he wrote them as a guage by which a Christian could measure his activities, I have taken the liberty to add a word or two and suggest they can also apply to goals.

Three Questions:
1. How will it affect me?
2. How will it affect others?
3. How will it affect the cause of Christ?
   Three Tests:
   1. Test of secrecy—is it all right if others know my goals?
   2. Test of universality—would it be all right for everyone else to have these goals?
   3. Test of prayer—were my goals born in prayer?

   Three Sources of Light:
   1. Light from within.
   2. Light from without (others).
   3. Light from above (God).[3]

The main goal of a Christian should not be to be a better Christian. Too selfish. Jesus said we should bear fruit, not be better fruit. We will not be better fruit unless we bear fruit. when we are not interested in others, we become self-centered. When we try to save ourselves, we lose ourselves. Only as we lose ourselves in service to him, can we please him. "He that winneth souls is wise" (Prov. 11:30).

Even a church should test its goals! One pastor became aware his church had no goals. Then he became convicted that the fault was not with the members, but himself. He prayed over the matter and God gave him four statements which he now places at the head of every job description. "The Philosophy of the Church," the pastor calls it. Notice how goals are built into it."

The church is the biggest business in the world, not one of the biggest businesses, but the biggest. Therefore, the church should be the best run business in the world, run more efficiently than any other.

The church should be the most honest business in the world, never teaching that it is all right for a worker, paid or unpaid, to do less than his best.

The purpose of the church is twofold, according to the Great Commission of Christ: (1) to win people to Christ, and (2) to teach them to do all things which Christ commanded them to do. People at the church now have goals in mind, and frequently speak of the exciting things God is doing.

Excitement is vitally related to goal-setting. And the excitement rapidly grows with goal reaching.

Ready for a dare? First, I dare you to ask God to give you some goals. Second, I dare you to apply the "Christian's Check List for Testing goals"—apply it to your goals until you can answer all seven questions in the affirmative. Third, I dare you to put your goals under the scrutiny of T. B. Maston's "Three Questions, Three Tests, and Three Sources of Light." Fourth, I dare you to try to keep from getting excited when God's enabling power works through you and you begin to see your (really his) goals reached.

---

[1] Clyde M. Narramore, *This Way to Happiness* (Grand Rapids: Zondervan Publishing Co., 1958), p. 156. Used by permission.

[2] Howard G. Hendricks, *Elijah* (Chicago: Moody Press, Moody Bible Institute, 1972), p. 19. Used by permission.

[3] Given in a lecture. Later Dr. Maston put his "Three Questions, Three Tests, and Three Sources of Light" in a book, *Right or Wrong* (Nashville: Broadman Press, 1955), pp. 29-46.

22
STRETCHING YOUR DREAMS

> Make no small plans; they have no power to move
> men's hearts. Unless our proposals are bold, they
> will be ineffective.
> —Elton Trueblood

> When the going gets tough, the tough get going.
> —Motto from football
> team's locker room.

Did you read about Mr. Miyamoto from Detroit? I like that fellow. Newspaper accounts recently said that for years this man had wanted to be a policemen, but he was too short. He would not be defeated. He tried every kind of stretching exercise he could imagine. He even had his wife put a bump on his head (most wives don't charge for that!). He said he gained an inch and a half. I'm not sure he made the police requirements, but a guy with zeal like that is hard to beat!

Stretching exercises! Who would have ever thought of that? That's ingenuity!

Many Christians are in desperate need of stretching. We're in the biggest business in the world, so it is imperative we be big thinkers.

While leading conferences for pastors in India in 1969, I heard one of the pastors share his opinion of American Christians. "You know what the problem with American Christians is? They think so small." Imagine someone being a small thinker in the world's biggest business!

"I Dare You to Stretch"

Satan is an expert in tempting us to withdraw into our little world and major on minors. Let the average Christian reach one other person for Christ in a year, and he is unbelievably content. If our minds were to begin to fathom the things God wants to accomplish through us, there would be no end to our excitement.

One day while thinking on my favorite verse, Ephesians 3:20, God hit me with an astounding thought-provoker. "Don't you see the challenge I am giving you?" God seemed to say. "You cannot out-ask me; you cannot out-think me; you cannot out-imagine me; you cannot out-dream me; you cannot out-do me, for I am able to do exceeding abundantly above all that you ask or think."

Incredible! But there was God daring me to think—daring me to stretch my imagination to the farthest limits—and then telling me he could still go beyond that. And that wasn't all—in the same verse he showed the way he would do it—"according to the power that worketh in us." Suddenly I saw it even clearer—he wanted to accomplish through us, according to the power he had already placed in us.

Force Yourself to New Thinking

Anyone who walks with God very closely for very long is going to be involved in a constant stretching process. The stretching will always begin in the mind.

The beginning concept will be for the believer to learn that God has no little assignments. That which seems small is extremely big because it is from God.

Where is the employer who hires a man and starts him moving mountains overnight! Rather, the employer starts him in a backroom somewhere and watches him tackle that assignment. But that backroom is one whale of a big assignment. If the trainee doesn't do that job right, he stays in the backroom from now on. Many a Christian feels unwanted because he thinks he's on God's third team. God has no third team. Everybody he saves is on his first team. If God assigns what seems to be a small task, let him remember the Employer is watching to see if he can do little things in a big way. Jesus said, "He that is faithful in that which is least, is faithful also in that which is much." God considers no assignment as a small one, but checks every job to see how it is done.

Another concept to quickly learn is that no one should ever wait for special assignments from God. Every believer knows five people he could reach for Christ. Those are his God-given assignments! He needs no further word from the Lord—Jesus said, "Ye shall be witnesses unto me!" By the time he wins those five, God will have put him in contact with five or ten others. The weekday world is literally loaded with assignments. Don't expect God to trust you with what you consider to be a giant need if you haven't even started on the sharing assignment He gave nearly 2,000 years ago.

You must also force yourself into exciting new thinking in the area of problems. God doesn't know a single problem he cannot turn into an opportunity. For centuries God has been taking what man considered as a problem and turning it into an opportunity—an opportunity for him to work a miracle. When we are going to stretch our imaginations to realize that the fulfillment of dreams begins with the problems that are right around us? When will we see through the eyes of eternity and view problems as opportunities?

"But you don't know the size of my problem. If you did, you wouldn't consider it an opportunity." No, but God knows the size of it. And he has handled problems a lot bigger than that. Problems are but opportunities in work-clothes, stepping stones to even greater-size victories.

Consider the greatest Christian you know. He has, no doubt, faced unbelievable obstacles all along the path. Long ago, however, he learned the lesson of taking those things immediately to God—not to the worry closet! Do you wonder why he possesses such peace?

"I have two things I can do with what appears to be a problem," the thrilled Christian says. "First, I can worry with it; second, I can trust it to God. If I worry, I am doubting God's ability to handle it; if I trust it to God, I have his promise he will give me the right solution in his timing (see Jas. 1:5-7)."

"Lord," he prays, "I thank you that even as I present this need to you that you are a miracle working God. I know that you know the answer and I trust it to you. I take it from my worry closet now, and by faith, I thrust it into your hands."

When David met Goliath, the shepherd boy looked at the giant and exclaimed, "The battle is the Lord's!" When Christ is enthroned, there is a new perspective on problems—the battle is the Lord's! Better yet, the battle is the Lord's and the thrill of victory is ours!

If your life is going to be stretched into the exciting life God wants it to be, you will be forced to always think of God as a big God able to meet big needs. Dr. Donald Grey Barnhouse tells of the day he was invited back to Princeton Theological Seminary to preach to the students, after being away for twelve years. One of his former Hebrew professors came to sit on the front row of Miller Chapel. At the close of the meeting, the old gentleman came by to comment. He remarked that he always tried to hear each former student once. "When I hear them, I know what their ministry will be," he commented. . . . "Some men have a little god and they are always in trouble with him. He can't do any miracles. He can't take care of the inspiration and transmission of the Scripture to us. He doesn't intervene on behalf of his people. They have a little God. . . .

"Then there are those who have a great God. He speaks and it is done. He commands and it stands fast. He knows how to show himself strong on behalf of them that fear him. You have a great God; and he will bless your ministry." Dr. Barnhouse said that old Dr. Wilson paused a moment, smiled, said, "God bless you," and walked out. [1]

A fifth bit of new thinking which will be required in God's stretching process is that we will learn to see blind alleys as bold challenges. There are two ways to view uncertainties—with fear and dread, or with the excitement of expectancy.

Practically no one wanted to go to Africa when C. T. Studd

left England to go in 1910. They had no idea what was out there! Mr. Studd saw it as an exciting challenge. His biography preserves these thrilling words: "Some wish to live within the sound, of Church or Chapel bell; I want to run a Rescue Shop, within a yard of hell." C. T.'s motto was: "If Jesus Christ be God, and died for me, then no sacrifice can be too great for me to make for him."

Contrast Abraham with the Israelites who followed Moses. Abraham left Ur of the Chaldees, and "went out, not knowing whither he went" (Heb. 11:8). The thrill of the unknown led him to become one of God's greatest men ever.

Those who left Egypt with Moses, on the other hand, could not stand uncertainties. When they heard the majority report of the committee which spied out Canaan, they gave up. "How oft did they provoke him in the wilderness, and grieve him in the desert. Yea, they turned back and limited the Holy One of Israel" (Ps. 78:41). They returned to the wilderness to die, even when the people in Canaan had already given up (Josh. 2:9-11). If only the Israelites had asked God to stretch their dreams, they would have discovered that blind alleys are in reality bold challenges.

If tomorrow's facts could all be known, life would be dull and routine, but the uncertainties of it all make for exciting opportunities. "I just can't wait to see what God wants to do with the new day" should be our constant thought.

Stretch Your Dreams into Realities

One of the toughest jobs we face is the task of discovering just exactly how to turn our dreams into realities.

Napoleon Hill, in his book, *Think and Grow Rich,* lists six steps which "turn desires into gold." I heard the pastor of a fast-growing church, Dr. Bob Moore, tell how application of these same principles (as he revised them to apply to his spiritual life) had greatly helped in goal-setting and goal-reaching. He dared us to try our hand at revisions, making spiritual application.

The six steps listed by Napoleon Hill are as follows:

1. Fix in your mind the exact amount of money you desire. It is not sufficient to say "I want plenty of money." Be definite as to the amount. (There is a psychological reason for definiteness which will be described in a subsequent chapter).
2. Determine exactly what you intend to give in return for the money you desire. (there is no such reality as "something for nothing.")
3. Establish a definite date when you intend to possess the money you desire.
4. Create a definite plan for carrying out your desire, and begin at once, whether you are ready or not, to put this plan into action.
5. Write out a clear, concise statement of the amount of money you intend to acquire, name the time limit for its acquisition, state what you intend to give in return for the money, and describe clearly the plan through which you intend to accumulate it.
6. Read your written statement aloud twice daily, once just before retiring at night, and once after arising in the morning. As you read—see and feel and believe yourself already in possession of the money.[2]

Now be realistic. If these six steps work in the financial area, would they not also (with slight revision) work in the spiritual area? Make your own revisions, or try mine—

1. Fix in your mind the exact goals (after prayer) you believe God would have you achieve. It is not sufficient to say, "I want to be a good Christian." Determine specifically what God has convinced you he wants you to do, and let those things be your goals.
2. Determine exactly how much of yourself you would be willing to give and how many sacrifices you would be willing to make to achieve the desires God has given you. God cannot honor the life which wants something for nothing. ("Faith is doing everything I can do and trusting God to do what I cannot do. God can do what I cannot do, but he will not do what I can do if I refuse to do it." [3])
3. Establish a definite date when you intend to possess the goals God has given you.
4. Create a definite plan for carrying out your desire, and begin at once, whether you are ready or not, to put the dreams God has given you into action.
5. Write out a clear, concise statement of the goals you intend to

acquire, name the time limit for the acquisition of these goals, state what you intend to give in return for the reaching of these goals, and describe clearly the plan for accomplishment.

6. Read your written statement aloud twice daily, praying about it, once just before retiring at night, and once after arising in the morning. As you read—see and feel and believe yourself already in possession of what God has revealed to you as his dream for your life. That's faith!

Don't listen to your doubts. Doubts will destroy what God wants to do through you. Remember that

if God gives the goal, and

if God wants you to reach it,

then God has a date in mind for the accomplishment
and God has a plan in mind as to how you can do
it,

then God would expect you to make sacrifices to attain
it

would want you to write it down and go to work on it

and would be thrilled if twice a day you envisioned him
doing it.

Stretch that imagination, and ask God to give you big dreams. "Lord, what would you like to see accomplished in the town where I live? What would you want achieved through my life? Let my imagination become a God-impressed goal factory. Even as you reveal goals you want me to have, I thank you that Christ in me has enough power to carry out those goals."

Human goals in the spiritual area will invariably be impressed by the negatives we've had since childhood, but divine goals could change the world.

---

[1] Barnhouse, *op. cit.*, pp. 132-33.

[2] Reprinted by permission of Hawthorn Books, Inc. from *Think and Grow Rich* by Napoleon Hill. Copyright © 1967, 1966, 1960, 1937 by The Napoleon Hill Foundation. All rights reserved.

[3] Hyles, *Blue Denim and Lace*, p. 172.

23
THE EXCITING ROLE OF FAITH

> The pilgrims, then, especially Christian, began to
> despond in his mind, and looked this way and that,
> but no way could be found by which they might
> escape the river. Then they asked the men if the
> waters were all of a depth. "No," said they, "you
> shall find it deeper or shallower as you believe
> in the King of the place."
>
> —John Bunyan
> *Pilgrim's Progress*

> All things are possible to him that believeth.
> —Jesus Christ

Faith is believing God. Someone has spoken of "the magic of believing." Faith is not magic but it works just that wonderfully. Faith is the one principle on the human side without which God will not move from the divine side.

What one word in the Bible separates the men from the boys? Faith. Why has God chosen to bless some of his people considerably more than others? Faith. What have the great achievers possessed in their makeup which most of us have missing from ours? Faith.

Faith, or the lack of it, is the stock-market barometer of our confidence. When our faith is right, we are right. We possess enthusiastic confidence, a God-given sense of expectancy, an inner peace which cannot be swayed by the circumstances of the moment.

Pick out the greatest Christian you know—and no doubt he excels in faith. Pick out the greatest Christian in Bible times—and faith was a dynamic he possessed.

Check your faith pulse? Are you satisfied with it? Has faith become a life-style for you?

Faith plays a giant part in success. If success is the continuing achievement of being the person God wants me to be, and the continuing achievement of established goals God helps me set, it is imperative I recognize the role of faith. In fact, I can ask God's guidance in giving me goals, I can write them on paper and read them aloud twice daily, I can even pray over them, but until I believe, nothing will happen.

Only when I believe do I begin to achieve.

The Importance of Faith

Earlier we noted the word "faith" is in the New Testament 234 times, and the word "believe" 251 times. Since "faith" and "believe" are from the exact same root in the original Greek (the only difference being in the verb or noun ending), then this one idea appears in the New Testament 485 times. This is astounding evidence that God places unusual importance as to where we stand in the arena of faith.

To read the New Testament record of Old Testament heroes is to again underline the emphasis of faith.

By faith, Abel	*By faith*, Abraham
By faith, Enoch	*By faith*, Joseph
By faith, Noah	*By faith*, Moses

are common expressions in the book of Hebrews. By faith the walls of Jericho fell, and through faith God's men have subdued kingdoms, wrought righteousness, obtained promises, and stopped the mouths of lions (Heb. 11:33).

From the lips of Jesus came frequent expressions about faith. "Verily I say unto you, If ye have faith as a grain of mustard seed . . . nothing shall be impossible unto you" (Matt. 17:20). "Therefore I say unto you, What things soever ye desire, when ye pray, believe that ye receive them, and ye shall have them" (Mark 11:24). "And all things, whatsoever ye shall ask in prayer, believing, ye shall receive" (Matt. 21:22). "Jesus said unto him, If thou canst believe, all things are possible to him that believeth" (Mark 9:23). "According to your faith be it unto you" (Matt. 9:29). "Great is thy faith: be it unto thee even as thou wilt" (Matt. 15:28).

From the other side, the Bible comments that "without faith it is impossible to please him" (Heb. 11:6). This is the victory that overcomes the world, even our faith (1 John 5:4). God provides the power which enables Spirit-filled believers to accomplish, but faith is the key which unlocks the power.

Faith is operative regardless.

> When everything about us seems downright bleak. . .
> When the heart is broken almost beyond repair
> When others would point us in another direction
> When needs are so gigantic as to be unreal
> When it seems Satan's whole army is marching against us
> When an inner voice says, "What's the use"
> When the understanding is unbelievably weak
> Faith goes right on.

Things don't change faith. Faith changes things. And the power of God is called on the scene.

The Definition of Faith

Hebrews 11:1 is excellent for its definition of faith. Try checking the verse in the different versions.

Kings James Version—Faith is the substance of things hoped for, the evidence of things not seen

American Standard Version—Now faith is assurance of things hoped for, a conviction of things not seen.

The Living Bible, Paraphrased—What is faith? It is the confident assurance that something we want is going to happen. It is the certainty that what we hope for is waiting for us, even though we cannot see it up ahead.

The Amplified Bible—Now faith is the assurance (the confirmation, the title-deed) of the things [we] hope for, being the proof of things [we] do not see and the conviction of their reality—faith perceiving as real fact what is not revealed to the senses.

Faith is complete confidence, wonderful assurance, seeing that which God has convinced us he wants us to accomplish as being accomplished. Faith is believing him so much that we believe he is definitely going to do it. Anyone can believe a previously established fact. Faith is believing the advanced assurance God has given us as much as we believe established fact.

Faith is envisioning—and here Webster's dictionary fits faith exactly—to have a mental image of, especially in advance of realization. How could you better describe faith? That's the quality God's great men have always possessed. They have looked to the future, seen God's goals, believed so much as to envision God accomplishing the task through them—and rejoiced both before and after God did it.

God's greats find a thrill in even thinking about faith. Trouble approaches, and it is but an opportunity for God to perform a miracle. A problem arises, and there is praise that God is doing such great things Satan had to attempt interference. A burden afflicts and prayer is offered, thanking God he is our great burden-bearer. Personal suffering approaches, only to find the believer saying, "Lord, I thank you that the sufferings of this world are not even worthy to be compared with the glory which shall be revealed hereafter" (see Rom. 8:18).

Believe God for the Big Thing

Had someone said to Caesar, "Speak to the Roman Senate over a radio—a machine that can throw your voice across the airwaves," Caesar would have said, "Impossible."

Had someone said to Homer, "Write your *Iliad* on a typewriter" and then explained it, Homer would have said, "Impossible."

Had someone said to Nero, "Ride from Naples to Rome in a machine that flies through the air," he would have said, "Impossible."

Had someone said to the Wright brothers, "A jet engine can carry your plane even faster," they would have thought, "Impossible."

History has now recorded that the very things thought impossible in centuries past are realities in our day. Things have a way of seeming impossible for awhile, and then some time passes, and God's man of accomplishment comes along.

If an ordinary person desires to be used of God and will pay the price to be used, God can afford to work through him with tremendous power.

We are too often content with little when God would give us much. Who said the great things of God have all been accomplished? In our hearts we should believe the best songs may yet be written; the best poems may yet be penned; the best sermons may yet be preached; the best lives may yet be lived; the best soul-winner may yet be found; the best man of faith may yet be uncovered. This is the most exciting day of history, but we must believe and achieve.

God wants you: Believe God for the big thing! God has so many lives he could change because of your life: Believe God for the big thing! God has dreams and goals he knows could be accomplished for his glory through your life: Believe God for the big thing!

Life is too short to be content with mediocrity. It is not enough to be what others are, or to do something because everybody is doing it. In the extraordinary age in which you live, when men are dreaming extraordinary dreams, carry life's Textbook by your side, and life's greatest companion in your heart as your constant source of strength, and—be something besides ordinary. Believe God for the big thing.

Noah dared to believe God for the big thing, and built an ark. But what if Noah had not? *Abraham* dared to believe God for the big thing, and left Ur not knowing whither he went. But what if Abraham had not? *Joseph* dared to believe God for the big thing, and believed God would deliver him from plots as well as prisons. But what if Joseph had not? *Moses* dared to believe God for the big thing, and headed toward Egypt to rescue the Jews. But what if Moses had not?

David dared to believe God for the big thing, and marched boldly out to meet Goliath. But what if David had not? *Heze-*

kiah dared to believe God for the big thing, and on his knees prayed for an extension of lifespan. But what if Hezekiah had not? *Jeremiah* dared to believe God for the big thing, and went out to buy a field to prove it. But what if Jeremiah had not?

Daniel dared to believe God for the big thing, and opened his windows three times a day to pray toward Jerusalem. But what if Daniel had not? *Shadrach, Meshach, and Abednego* dared to believe God for the big thing, and asked him for protection from a burning fiery furnace. But what if they had not? If these men had not believed God for the big thing, God would never have worked the big thing in their lives. Someone else might have stepped in willing to be used, but these would have been forgotten and buried in the sands of time.

Attacks on Faith

Faith is positive; hence, negatives will attack and seek to destroy it.

C. S. Lovett tells of the time he and Dewey Lockman and Dr. Franklin Logsdon went to see Dr. Charles E. Fuller, preacher on the "Old Fashioned Revival Hour." In the course of the conversation, the name of a prominent Christian leader was mentioned, one who was then attacking Fuller Seminary. "I shall never forget Brother Fuller's response to the comment this man made about his school.

" 'Yeeesss,' he drawled, 'God bless him.'

"Dr. Logsdon was the quickest to respond, 'You don't seem too upset, Brother Fuller!'

"Then came an astonishing reply: 'Why should I let someone else decide how I am going to act!' " [1]

When faith gets attacked, it will often be attacked by temper, or hatred, or strife, and just enough to give you a good case of the "disgruntleds." Just enough to block all your advances in the area of faith.

Watch for the negatives. A sign appeared on a city bus

in downtown New York: "Doctors tell us that hating people can cause: ulcers, heart attacks, headaches, skin rashes, high blood pressure, and asthma." Someone had scrawled beneath it, "It doesn't make the people you hate feel good either."

Faith is the road to big things; hence, fear will seek to destroy it.

Fear makes faith flounder. Faith that flounders has lost its power and, of course, accomplishes nothing. Floundering faith will appear to be going somewhere and of course, goes nowhere. God cannot bless a life once fear has occupied God's throne chair. "God hath not given us the spirit of fear," Paul admonishes Timothy, "but of power, and of love, and of a sound mind" (2 Tim. 1:7).

Faith is the road to success; hence, defeated friends will seek to sidetrack you.

When God wishes to do something big, he often gives the dream to only one person. If that one person gets defeated, the God-given dream is gone. Jack Taylor has wisely admonished, "If Satan cannot defeat you, he will defeat someone whose defeat will defeat you." The attack on faith may come from well-meaning friends who simply have no desire to be used of God themselves, or even from family members. The one who walks by faith must expect to sometimes walk all alone.

Faith refuses to base itself on feelings; hence, feelings will attack from all sides.

Great Christians refuse to major on feelings. They major on faith. Any Christian always interested in his feelings will never amount to much for God. Until he gets his eyes off himself and on Christ and a needy world, he will miss all the big goals God has for him. When Thomas said, "If I can see, I'll believe"; he was not exercising faith, but doubt. When a Christian moves by feelings instead of by faith, he too has chosen to exercise doubt.

Faith refuses to acknowledge doubt; hence, doubt does everything possible to gain inroads through the questioning pro-

cess.

Just about the time you've set your goals, stretched your dreams, and begun to believe God for big things, expect to be attacked on all sides by questions. "What have I gotten myself into?" "What if it doesn't work? Wow, am I in trouble!" "Do you suppose God intended that job for someone else, and I just thought it was for me?" Always remember, if God gave you those goals after prayer, then faith will look far beyond all question marks and believe.

When that happens, extraordinary power will begin to flow.

---

[1] C. S. Lovett, *Unequally Yoked Wives* (Baldwin Park, Calif.: Personal Christianity Publishers, 1968), pp. 71-72.

24
EXPERIMENT STATIONS AND
RESEARCH CENTERS

> The Lord Jesus claims the use of your body, your
> whole being, your complete personality, so that
> as you give yourself to him through the eternal
> Spirit, he may give himself to you through the
> eternal Spirit, that all your activity as a human
> being on earth may be his activity in and through
> you; that every step you take, every word you
> speak, everything you do, everything you are, may
> be an expression of the Son of God, in you as
> man.[1]
>
> —W. Ian Thomas

> We must look out that our humility is not in-
> dolence with a solemn countenance upon it, the
> real fact being that we are content with the lowest
> place in heaven because we have not energy and
> self-sacrifice enough to make us strive after the
> highest.[2]
>
> —A. J. Gordon

Our age is the age of science. In the days we have been
alive, God has taught us a thousand things from his vast
storehouse of knowledge. One of the sidelights of scientific
advancement has been the discovery of the thrill involved in
research and experimentation. Reflection will reveal:

For the sake of science, test pilots have tested the heav-
ens—higher, higher, and still higher.

For the sake of science, astronomers have counted their lives
as nothing, but have given themselves to scan the stars a
thousand nights.

For the sake of science, mathematicians have created advanced math, talked in new terminology, wrestled new for-
mulas into being so man could scan the stars.

For the sake of science, many a man has dedicated himself

to be hidden 12 hours a day in a research laboratory, simply to uncover secrets heretofore unknown.

For the sake of science, astronauts have been shot into space with the thrust of unbelievably powerful missiles right beneath their spaceship.

For the sake of science, men have become human guinea pigs to stay in space for heretofore untested lengths of time to see what heretofore impossible tasks could be accomplished out there.

For the sake of science, men have walked on the moon, and the volunteers to go have always exceeded the number needed.

Risk is not considered important. Man apparently has no hesitation in becoming a personalized research center—regardless of the cost. In fact, it would seem in most cases the higher the risk involved, the more volunteers. There is something daringly wonderful about being in experimental work. The dedicated scientist seems to say. "Whether I live or die is not important, but the advancement of science is all that matters. If I can but add to the progress of mankind, my life will not have been in vain."

Why has science advanced so fast? Because of these personalized research centers.

Abundance of Surprises

When a child of God, filled with the Spirit, begins to allow God to stretch his dreams, and ventures boldly into the arena of faith excitingly believing God, he is in for an abundance of surprises.

One surprise is the excitement of newly discovered power. No longer is he someone trying to do something for God. He is now someone who is trusting God to do something through him. Boundaries change. No longer is he limited to what he can accomplish in human strength. Now he will discover what God can accomplish with divine strength. He discovers it is "not me" but "Christ in me," not "my weakness" but "his strength," not "my problems" but "his opportunities," not "my needs" but "his inexhaustible storehouse of supply."

Another surprise is the excitement of new eyesight. He trades in the old eyes of human vision, and begins to see things through God's eyes. "For we walk by faith, not by sight." Faith is a far better set of glasses than the believer has ever known before. Twenty-twenty vision can only satisfy until a believer knows there is something even better. What a blessing the day he tires of living by feeling and begins the new adventure of living by faith!

Another surprise is that the promises of God come fantastically alive. Promises heretofore hidden become treasure-chests, and each day unveils a new promise from God's thousands in his Word. The Bible is no longer just history. It is His-story. The promises become as up-to-date as the morning newspaper. A promise made in the first century becomes wonderfully applicable in the twentieth century.

Still a bigger surprise is the way boredom changes to excitement. In the twentieth century B.C.E. (Before Christ Enthroned), spiritual monotony and boredom carried the day—

Church had been a drudgery. He soon discovered it was not quite so bad if he missed one Sunday out of three. Sunday night was out of the question. A later revelation which came to him was that if he would turn on the television and be able to tell his friends he heard a sermon on television, he could miss three Sundays out of four, and have a good excuse for it all. He didn't have to tell them he read the funnies, drank his coffee, and shaved all while the sermon was on.

Twentieth century A.C.E. (After Christ Enthroned) is a different story. The believer now sees himself in a new light and every day carries the potential of new thrill. He says: Jesus Christ lives in me through his Holy Spirit. He is eager to show me what he can accomplish through my life. My body is the dwelling place he has chosen to live in. My role is a new one now. I am his experiment station, his research center. What he wishes to accomplish in this world he may wish to accomplish through me.

The Believer a Research Center

I am his research center! Not that God needs to travel down new roads. He had been there before. But day by day he would allow me to walk down new paths of usefulness to him. "Hey, that's exciting. God, you mean you would use me!"

Of course he will use you! If you're usable. Why do you suppose he came to live in your life through the Holy Spirit? He has taken up residence inside. He is Lord of the life, wanting to use the life to the maximum.

Every believer should be God's personal research center and experiment station. When Paul shared with the Colossians that "Christ [is] in you, the hope of glory," he quickly became more specific saying, "Christ worketh in me mightily" (Col. 1:27,29).

Abraham readily threw a knapsack on his back and headed out from his home to become an experiment station. Through his life God would show how many blessings can come to the man of faith.

Moses submitted to God to become an experiment station in the presence of Pharaoh himself. Through his life Egypt for generations would remember the power of one man plus God.

Joshua didn't care who laughed when he shared his battle plan for conquering Jericho. He believed he was to be God's experiment station for conquering the Promised Land.

Rahab, sick of sin, turned to God and allowed him to show the world how God could even change a harlot.

Ruth bravely put her neck on the line to pave the way for her Gentile world to follow the true God.

Elijah experimented with challenging idolatry. He allowed God to use him to walk boldly into the enemy camp and challenge Baal worship in a Mount Carmel Super Bowl.

Daniel thrilled when God chose him to answer the question, "What's a man of God to do in a lion's den?"

The Hebrew children became personal research centers for the article, "How to Walk Through a Fiery Furnace."

Peter experimented with using simple testimony and preaching to foreign people who gathered in Jerusalem for the Jewish feast day of Pentecost.

Paul became God's guinea pig for first-century missionary work. He asked Christ to use him to share hundreds of miles away from Tarsus. He was not even afraid to go to Rome.

Barnabas researched how to help discouraged young men like John Mark regain their composure and become giants for God.

Dwight Moody explored Sunday School work among needy kids of Chicago. An experiment in how to make godly usage of adversity and prison cells was John Bunyan's project. David Livingstone became a research center to explore the exciting villages of Africa where no white man had ever been. William Carey so had Christ in his heart he headed for India and became a pioneer in Bible translation of various languages and dialects. Bill Borden of Yale (1909) dreamed not of the million dollars he had in the bank but of sharing Christ among Muslims on the other side of the world.

All of these simply discovered that the most exciting thing in the world is to have God use you. There is no life more adventuresome than that of the believer who can say with Paul, "Christ is in me, and works in me mightily."

Rules for the Research Center

1. God utilizes no draftees. He calls, but all who are to have his power working through them are strictly volunteers.
2. Those used today are not certain of being used tomorrow. Before a vessel can be used, it must be "clean, fit for the Master's use."
3. God shares his glory with no man. The one who is used of God and then takes credit and praise for doing what God did may well be overlooked in the days ahead.
4. God always provides his power when man is ready for it.

The person who believes opportunities are "passing him by" needs to reassess whether he is totally yielded to God's control. The same one who believes the "harvest is white, but the labourers are few" is not about to overlook usable instruments. He has never overlooked even one.

Excitement That Endures

Occasionally someone may question whether it pays to serve Jesus. Youth might ask, "What's in it for me? Suppose I do become God's research center and allow him to accomplish his will in my life, what can I expect?"

Not long ago I sat in the home of a retired minister in East Missouri. Excited, loaded with enthusiasm, yet already more than fourscore years of age, Forrest Lowry loves to tell of his daily thrills. Many days he is not able to visit others but he exclaims, "You know, I just tell the Lord to send the needy to my door and he does. I can't wait to see who is coming next!"

"You know," Dr. Lowry continued, "the devil doesn't have any happy old people. I've never seen a one."

My mind reverted to years I spent on Seminary Hill in Fort Worth. The young people were excited, thrilled, having fun, serving as research centers, preparing to go out to serve Jesus Christ around the world. However, the 1,600 or 1,800 youth around the campus were not the ones with greatest joy. One group on campus amazed everyone.

The group? They were the missionaries who had retired after 30 or 40 years of service in some foreign country. They would drift back to Seminary Hill, and rent homes within walking distance. Most every day they would show up at the chapel service, or visit in the classrooms, or relax in the Student Center. They were the troops who had pioneered in the hard countries—the difficult areas—where the going had been unbelievably tough. Yet there they were, the most excited group I've ever seen.

Put it all together. Serving as an experiment station for Jesus

Christ allows one to come to the end of life with thrill and joy. Whether twenty-five or eighty-five, every day is an exciting prayer: "Father, just think—a brand new day. I face this day with the awareness that Jesus Christ is alive in my life. Christ liveth in me! Lord, what would you like to see accomplished in the town where I live today? I am your research center.

> Walk through my feet—
> Work through my hands—
> Think through my brain—
> Speak through my lips—
> Win through my sharing—

I am yours, Lord. Meet needs, lift burdens, bring joy, save souls today as you work through me. I cannot do it, but you can. I am not able, but you are. I do not have the ability, but you do. And I thank you that you live in me, and desire to work in my life today."

Game Plan

Success is being what God wants me to be, and achieving what God wants me to achieve. It is only natural to expect there should be a "Game Plan" for achievement.

G   God's Fullness. So as not to work in human power, so as not to be just what I can be in human strength, but so I can be all I can be in his strength, I must have God's fullness, the daily infilling of his Spirit, the daily cleansing he provides, the daily leadership he provides as he occupies the throne chair in my life.

A   Aims. These are the goals. Once I thought of my goals. No more. His goals are the only ones that can build a better world.

M   Motivation. Christ is not just in me to be, but in me to do. When I have exhaled (thrust out the old, the sinful, the smudged page) and put it under his cross, I can believe the magnificent promise of 1 John

1:9. When I have spiritually inhaled, I have made the new surrender of the throne chair to Christ, gained anew the realization he knows how to direct the life much better than I do. Now from within he motivates, excites my spirit, counts my problems his opportunities, shares in response to my asking his desires for the day, his power to accomplish.

E   Envision. By faith I can believe that what he challenges me to do, he is able to get done. Failure is not his motto. Self fails, but Christ succeeds. Now I can look at the challenge he assigned, and envision the goal being reached, the assignment carried out. Through the eyes of faith I can see it achieved.

There's the game plan. He's the coach. I'm excited about that. But there's more. He has allowed me to be on the team. In the most thrilling day of history, I'm on the team. In the day of the most challenges ever, I'm on the team. In the day when the opponent is displaying unusual toughness, I'm on the team. In that day the coach has sent me in to play. In the day when it seems God has chosen to manifest his might more than ever before, I'm on the team.

Perhaps once you said, "God chose me?" There need be no doubt about that. He put you here, didn't he? He matched you with this generation, didn't he? Turn your question mark to an exciting exclamation point, "God chose me!"

Don't you want in on what God is up to? He says, "You can. That's why I put you here. Have a go at it!"

Caution Lights in Usefulness

1. Don't miss the main assignment. We are not filled with God's power to neglect the main assignment. The main assignment given to believers is in Matthew 28:19-20 and Acts 1:8. Less than 24 hours prior to Calvary, Jesus stated one truth three different times: "He that abideth in me, and I in him the same bringeth forth much fruit" (John 15:6). "Herein is

my Father glorified, that ye bear much fruit; so shall ye be my disciples" (v. 8). "Ye have not chosen me, but I have chosen you, and ordained you, that ye should go and bring forth fruit, and that your fruit should remain" (v. 16). Sharing Christ with others has to occupy prime importance in the life of the believer.

2. No believer is stronger than his prayer life. Victories are won in the prayer closet. "Without me ye can do nothing" (John 15:5) means that Satan would do everything possible to keep you from daily prayer appointments with God or to hinder your mind while praying.

3. Stay in the Word of God.—"Faith cometh by hearing, and hearing by the Word of God" (Rom. 10:17). God simply cannot use Christians as research centers regularly who neglect his Word.

4. Major on faith, not feeling. Satan is a past master at moving emotions. Do not assume emotional jags mean God had chosen to use you. A wise man stated, "God expects spiritual fruit, not religious nuts." Rely on the promises of God and allow him to use you to reach others for his glory.

5. God can accomplish much more through an army than through an individual. Occasionally, a Christian gets to feeling his importance and senses he doesn't need the local church. You may not need your church, but you need some church. Find a church where the Bible is preached, and believed, and where Christians radiate Christ in everyday excitement. But by all means have a church! Of the more than 100 times the word "church" is used in the New Testament, more than 90 of these usages refer to a specific local church in a specific local setting. Christians are involved in a war with the devil, and watch out when the devil tries to get you to be a one-man army!

6. Expect God to use you if you are Spirit-filled. It is an astounding fact that some people sell out to Christ and then seem surprised that God would use them. Expect him to use the available, usable tool. God never runs out of job assign-

ments. When you are not being used, don't doubt God. Remember, "Get usable and the Lord will wear you out."

---

[1] W. Ian Thomas, *The Saving Life of Christ* (Grand Rapids: Zondervan Publishing Co., 1962), p. 151. Used by permission.

[2] A. J. Gordon, *Great Pulpit Masters Series, Vol. VIII* (New York: Fleming H. Revell Co., 1951), p. 66.

CONCLUSION

25
THE WORLD'S GREATEST SUCCESS STORY—AND YOU

> You can find fault with Moses, and with Abram, and with Job, and with Isaiah, and with David, and with Paul, and with Barnabas. You can put your finger on the defects of men up and down the world, without any exception; but Christ alone stands flawless, spotless, and without sin. You cannot say that about any other life. His life attests his divine claims.
>
> —George W. Truett

> Other men are great artists or poets or generals or statesmen, whereas Jesus is a great man. His greatness lies in the realm of personality, in the kingdom of character. His achievement was not wrought with paint or with chisel or with sword or with pen, but by the heavenly magic of a victorious will.
>
> —Charles Edward Jefferson

A book on success and motivation should fittingly conclude with a chapter on Jesus. No one has ever mastered those subjects to the extent Jesus did. He knew more about success, motivated more people, and personally embodied the fullness of God's Spirit more than any man who has ever lived.

Success Personified

Study the idea of success. History would testify that Jesus has definitely proved more successful with his life and teachings than any other. Men have bestowed an abundance of titles on Jesus, but one more needs to be added. Jesus was a success.

Remember the definition? Success is the continuing achievement of being the person God wants me to be, and the continuing achievement of established goals God helps set. That definition was perfectly fulfilled in the thirty-three short years of Jesus' life. He continually reached that achievement of being the person God wanted him to be. Not once did he fail. In addition, he continually achieved the goals God helped him set. Frequently he was tempted to turn aside and formulate some selfish goals. He steadfastly refused. Only the goals God wanted accomplished in his life were deemed worthy of his acceptance.

While he lived, men listened to his magnificent teaching and exclaimed, "Never man so spake." Ever since his death, men have been studying his life only to conclude, "Never man so lived."

Napoleon said, "I know men; and I tell you that Jesus Christ is no mere man. Between him and every other person in the world there is no possible term of comparison. Alexander, Caesar, Charlemagne, and I have founded empires. But on what did we rest the creations of our genius? Upon force. Jesus Christ founded his empire upon love; and at this hour millions of men would die for him." [1]

Herbert Lockyer remarks: "He never wrote a book, and yet all the libraries of the country could not hold the books that have been written about him. He never wrote a song, and yet he has furnished the theme for more songs than all the song writers combined. He never founded a college, but all the schools put together cannot boast of having as many students." [2]

"The Man Christ" is the title of some succinct comments by Therese Lindsey:

> He built no temple, yet the farthest sea
> Can yield no shore that's barren to His place
> For bended knee.

> He wrote no book, and yet His words and prayer
> Are intimate on many, myriad tongues,
> Are counsel everywhere.

> The life He lived has never been assailed,

Nor any precept, as He lived it, yet
Has ever failed.

He built no kingdom, yet a King from youth
He reigned, is reigning yet; they call His realm
The Kingdom of the Truth.[3]

Motivation Expert

Bruce Barton shares his opinion of the motivating ability of Jesus in *The Man and the Book Nobody Knows.*

He did not overthrow the oppressive government of Rome. He did not lower the tax rate. He did not improve sanitary conditions in Jerusalem, nor did he erect a public library in Nazareth. He did not increase the wages of Christians over those of infidels. He taught no sure cure for disease. The economic status of his followers was exactly as it had been: He found them fishermen, he left them fishermen. . . .

But his fishermen were different men, transformed, endowed with power, capable of great faith and magnificent achievement. Through them and their successors He started more philanthropies than all others who have ever lived. Hospitals and clinics, charities and libraries, schools and colleges have multiplied where he has inspired the souls of men. His religion is the best asset of civilization. That part of the world outside of which very few of us would willingly spend our days is named for him, Christendom.[4]

Without a doubt, the master motivator of all time has been Jesus of Nazareth. Others have spoken of doing it, but Jesus did it and continues to do it. He has instilled more confidence, brought more joy, thrilled more lives, excited more hearts, and moved more men to action than any other man who has ever lived.

Motivation is never automatic. The man who is not motivated cannot motivate. The one who is not moved to action himself is not going to move anyone else to action, at least not for long. The question worth asking is, "Who motivated the earthly Jesus?" What was there about Jesus that set him aside from the crowd? What gave him the qualities he possessed? What made him

Confident
  A dreamer
    A master motivator
      An extraordinary goal-achiever
      Filled with the power of God
      A personality who drew great crowds
    Loaded with love
Yet bold and brave?
That question is just about to be answered.

Filled with the Spirit

Now the secret can be shared. The most successful person who ever lived was also the most Spirit-filled person. From the outset of his public ministry, the Bible indicates Jesus was filled with the Holy Spirit. Luke records, "And Jesus being full of the Holy Spirit returned from Jordan, and was led by the Spirit into the wilderness" (Luke 4:1). After the temptations the secret is again shared—"And Jesus returned in the power of the Spirit into Galilee" (v. 14). When he came to Nazareth after he began his public ministry, he went into the synagogue, and the passage he chose to read began, "The Spirit of the Lord is upon me" (v. 18).

Years later, with Jesus long since gone, the writer of Acts mentions "How God anointed Jesus of Nazareth with the Holy Ghost and with power; who went about doing good, and healing all that were oppressed of the devil: for God was with him" (Acts 10:38).

Do You Have What It Takes?

Success that will last is what every man needs. So stop being content with being Mr. Average, and determine to be the achiever God intends. A good spelling of success is

     S   Spirit-filled
     U   Usable
     C   Courageous

C   Confident
E   Enthusiastic
S   Submitted
S   Success-oriented

SPIRIT-FILLED. Jesus stayed alone in prayer until the power of God literally absorbed every portion of his life. He was never anxious to just attract the multitudes. He was anxious to be totally absorbed with the power of God. If needs be, he would leave thousands to push apart, go across the lake and find a place to pray.

USABLE. Jesus determined to be a vessel, clean, fit for the Father's use. "He was tempted in all points like as we are, yet without sin" (Heb. 4:15). Is it any wonder God could use him? The unusual thing would have been for God not to use him. The natural thing for God is to always use the usable vessel.

COURAGEOUS. Money changers with exorbitant interest rates had best stay out of the Temple area when Jesus came to town, for he always possessed an abundance of courage. When he felt something was God's will, he would move into the arena of battle to accomplish it.

CONFIDENT. Jesus never lacked confidence. He believed he could, by the power of God, accomplish exactly what God wanted him to accomplish. Not once did Jesus move about with indecisiveness. Because he knew his heart was right and his goals were right, he moved about with unswerving confidence.

ENTHUSIASTIC. The root of "enthusiasm" is the Greek word *enthousiasmos*. This word comes from two smaller Greek words, *en theos*, meaning "in God." The greatest kind of enthusiasm comes when one knows he is "in God." There is deep inner excitement and thrill. Jesus possessed a fantastic enthusiasm not only to live the abundant life, but to share it.

SUBMITTED. One reason God could afford to fill Jesus with power was because Jesus was totally submitted to the will of God. The person who is not submissive will be put on the shelf. God has a way of simply moving on by that person to use another. A study of the prayer Jesus prayed in Gethsemane is an excellent example of total submission.

SUCCESS-ORIENTED. Whether or not the desire to be successful is helpful depends completely upon the definition. To Jesus success was being the person God intended for him to be, and achieving the goals God intended that he achieve. Everything Jesus did was oriented in this one basic context. Having set his goals in the place of prayer, he would refuse to be satisfied until each one was accomplished. A Bible concordance will reveal that the word "must" was an oft-used word in his vocabulary. At age twelve the impelling inner drive was "I must be about my Father's business." When one says "must" as Jesus frequently did, it is an indication that goals are set, eyes will not be turned aside, and the person is goal-oriented toward successful achievement. It is time we learned that
when one can enjoy life, as Jesus did,
    help people on every hand, as Jesus did,
        lift hundreds out of defeat, as Jesus did,
        lead others to a right relationship with God, as Jesus did
    and hear God say he is well-pleased, as Jesus did,
then that one has discovered the true meaning of success!

Someone may wonder, "Yes, but do I have what it takes to start down the road of success and begin to apply the principles found in this book?" To every person who has come to know Christ in a personal way the answer is a resounding yes. There are two reasons why. One is because of who he is. The other is because of his relationship to you.

An unknown author wrote, "Nineteen centuries have come and gone, and today Jesus is the centerpiece of the human race, and the leader of all human progress. I am well within the mark when I say that all the armies that ever marched, all the navies that were ever built, all the parliaments that have ever sat, and all the kings that have ever ruled put together have not affected the life of man upon this earth like this one solitary personality."

This man Jesus knew where he was going. He was loaded with initiative, drive, accomplishment, desire, confidence, appeal to the masses, and goal-reaching. Even in his last year on earth, he said, "Ye shall be witnesses unto me." Still nearly 2,000 years later, millions have dedicated themselves to do exactly as he asked them to do. If there was ever anyone who was a master of the success area, it was the Man of Galilee.

And just think, he is in you!

---

[1] Frank S. Mead (ed.), *Encyclopedia of Religious Quotations* (New York: Revell, 1965), p. 56.

[2] Herbert Lockyer, *The Man Who Changed the World*, Vol. I (Grand Rapids: Zondervan Publishing Co., 1967), p. 24. Used by permission.

[3] Poem by Therese Lindsey, taken from *Christ and the Fine Arts* by Cynthia Pearl Maus (New York: Harper & Brothers, 1938), p. 3.

[4] Bruce Barton, *The Man and the Book Nobody Knows* (New York: The Bobbs-Merrill Co., 1924, 1925, 1929, 1956, 1959), p. 214. Used by permission.